Triceratops

and other Cretaceous Plant-Eaters

by Daniel Cohen

Capstone Press

MINNEAPOLIS

Printed in the United States of America.

Capstone Press • 2440 Fernbrook Lane • Minneapolis, MN 55447

Editorial Director   John Coughlan
Managing Editor   Tom Streissguth
Production Editor   James Stapleton
Book Design   Timothy Halldin

Library of Congress Cataloging-in-Publication Data

Cohen , Daniel, 1936-
   Triceratops and other Cretaceous plant-eaters/Daniel Cohen
    p. cm. -- (Dinosaurs of North America)
    Includes bibliographical references (p. 41) and index.
    Summary: Describes what is known about three different types of dinosaurs that lived in parts of the United States and Canada from 140 to 65 million years ago.
   ISBN 1-56065-289-6
    1. Triceratops--Juvenile literature. 2. Parasaurolophus--Juvenile literature. 3. Maiasaura--Juvenile literature.
[1. Triceratops. 2. Parasaurolophus. 3. Maiasaura.
4. Dinosaurs.] I. Title. II. Series: Cohen, Daniel, 1936-
Dinosaurs of North America.
QE862.O65C63 1996
567.9'7--dc20   95-11244
                                  CIP
                                  AC

Table of Contents

Chapter 1
When They Lived

Millions and millions of years ago, huge herds of horned and duck-billed dinosaurs roamed what is now the North American continent. These **herbivorous** (plant-eating) dinosaurs were pursued by the largest, fiercest **carnivorous** (meat-eating) dinosaurs the world had ever known.

Then, quite suddenly, all of the dinosaurs were gone. Why? Was the earth struck by **asteroids** or a giant **comet**? Did a nearby star explode? No one knows.

Most of the **species** that have ever existed on earth are now gone. Species become extinct

Quaternary Age
1.8m to present

65m   Tertiary Age   1.8m

140m Cretaceous Age 65m

195m Jurassic Age   140m

230m Triassic Age   195m

280m Permian Age 230m

345m Carboniferous 280m

395m Devonian Age 345m

435m Silurian Age   395m

500m Ordovcian Age 435m

700m Cambrian Age 500m

} **Birds**
Mammals

} **Reptiles**
Amphibians

} **Fish**
Primitive chordate

and new ones evolve to take their place. But the sudden extinction of so many different species that had been so successful for so long seems unnatural.

The speculation on what happened continues. And it will continue for a long time. All we know for certain is that 65 million years ago, the dinosaurs that had dominated the earth disappeared.

Paleontologists–scientists who study ancient life on earth–divide the history of life into three great eras. They are the **Paleozoic** (pail-ee-oh-ZO-ic), or ancient life, era; the **Mesozoic** (mez-oh-ZO-ic), or middle life, era; and the **Cenozoic** (sen-oh-ZO-ic), or recent life, era.

The dinosaurs lived during the Mesozoic era, which is often called the Age of Dinosaurs. The Mesozoic era itself is divided into three periods. First is the **Triassic** (try-ASS-ic) period, from 230 million to 195 million years ago. Dinosaurs first began to appear late in the Triassic period.

The next period was the **Jurassic** (joo-RASS-ic) period, from 195 million to 140 million years ago. Dinosaurs flourished during this period, and the largest dinosaurs in history lived during this time.

The third period was the **Cretaceous** (cret-AY-shus) period, from 140 million to 65 million years ago. New types of dinosaurs appeared and the creatures were more numerous and successful than ever before.

A paleontologist studies skeletons, fossils, and other remains of prehistoric life.

The Cretaceous period was a time of great change on the earth. At one time, all of the earth's land mass was clumped together in a single supercontinent. This land mass began to split apart during the Jurassic period. This split accelerated during the Cretaceous period.

The Cretaceous period was also a time of enormous volcanic upheaval. Mountain ranges appeared and new islands were formed. The earth's climate changed dramatically as well. The seasons became more pronounced. There were more storms. The moist and tropical conditions of the Jurassic period no longer prevailed over the entire earth.

The drifting of the continents, the formation of mountain ranges, and the harsher climate meant that dinosaurs could no longer freely roam the world. The range of many of the later Cretaceous dinosaurs was more limited than it had been during the Jurassic period.

As the earth changed, so did the animals and plants. Early in dinosaur history, the creatures ate mainly ferns, palms, and cycads, which are

primitive plants. By the late Cretaceous period, flowering plants and trees had evolved. Oaks, hickories, and other tree families began to appear in cooler areas where the more primitive plants could not survive.

New species of turtles, snakes, and other reptiles developed. Amphibians like frogs and salamanders first appeared during the Cretaceous period. Herons, gulls, and plovers, birds that evolved during the Cretaceous, are still familiar today.

A Maiasaura, whose name means good mother lizard, tends its nest of young.

Mammals and dinosaurs had evolved at about the same time during the Triassic period. The mammals continued to thrive during the Cretaceous period, but they remained small. They had changed very little from the mammals of earlier times. They would not really develop or dominate until the dinosaurs became extinct.

That brings us back to the question of the extinction of the dinosaurs at the end of the Cretaceous period. While the earth had certainly changed during this period, the dinosaurs appeared able to adapt well to the changes. New species of dinosaurs evolved to take advantage of the changing conditions.

Then, at the end of the Cretaceous period, all the dinosaurs suddenly died out. This appears to have happened very quickly. Though many theories about the extinction of the dinosaurs have been offered by scientists, there is no universal agreement on what happened. The extinction of the dinosaurs remains one of the most puzzling mysteries of science.

Ceratopsian mouths were perfect for plant eating

Triceratops

(try-SER-ah-tops)
three-horned face
Range*: Western United States and Canada*
Length*: 30 feet (9 meters)*
Weight*: 6 tons (5.4 metric tons)*

The most common large plant-eating dinosaurs of the late Cretaceous period in western North America were the **ceratopsids** (ser-a-TOP-sids). They were found nowhere else in the world.

The word, which means horn faced, fits these massive four-legged dinosaurs. They had huge heads, and a bony frill, developed from the rear skull bones, protected their neck. Different species had from one to a dozen

A Triceratops had only its bony horns to defend itself against the powerful Tyrannosaurus rex.

sharp horns growing from their snout, head, or from the bony frill.

The pillarlike legs and heavy, hoofed feet supported a stocky body that was covered with a tough, thick hide. Scientists now believe that

these dinosaurs could run at speeds of up to 30 miles (48 kilometers) per hour, at least for a short distance. The modern animal they resemble most is the rhinoceros. But the dinosaurs were much bigger.

A charging dinosaur of this type would have been a terrifying foe. In that time, dinosaurs needed all the protection they could get. The Cretaceous world was a dangerous one.

All the evidence suggests that these dinosaurs found safety in numbers. They moved in great herds through the forests. When threatened by some of the great predators of the period, like Tyrannosaurus, they could have formed a circle with their horned heads facing outward toward the danger. The smaller and weaker young would be in the center. That would have been an effective defense, even against the fearsome Tyrannosaurus.

These dinosaurs did not have teeth. They foraged through the upland forests chopping off vegetation with their sharp, toothless, beaklike mouths. They adapted to take advantage of the newly evolved and tougher vegetation of the late Cretaceous.

Of all the horned dinosaurs, the best known, and probably the most numerous, was Triceratops. It was also the largest dinosaur of

Triceratops had a huge head and a bony frill that protected the neck.

this type. A full-grown Triceratops weighed more than a modern African bull elephant, today's largest land animal. Its skull alone, with its short neck frill, was more than six feet (1.8 meters) long. It had a short, thick nose horn and two long horns higher on its head.

These horns could have measured more than three feet (90 centimeters) each.

Scientists were confused when the first fragmentary remains of this creature were discovered. When the great fossil collector Othniel Charles Marsh was shown the horns of a Triceratops, he thought they belonged to an

extinct species of buffalo. Marsh was wrong. A few years later one of his associates found a full skull of one of the creatures. Marsh realized the horns came from a long-extinct dinosaur, not a dead buffalo.

Because of the massive structure of Triceratops's skull, it was more likely to be preserved than the bones of other, weaker dinosaurs. Hundreds of well-preserved Triceratops specimens have been found over the years in the western United States and Canada. The American fossil hunter Barnum Brown is said to have collected more than 500 skulls of this particular dinosaur. Today more than 15 species of Triceratops are recognized. Fossilized remains of this dinosaur can be found in most large and many small museum collections.

Many of the skulls, horns, and neck frills were found to be damaged and scarred. This suggests that individual Triceratops often sparred with one another. Perhaps they locked horns and shoved one another with their head

shields, rather than doing actual damage with their sharp horns. These dangerous weapons were probably only used on real enemies like Tyrannosaurus.

Fossils show that Triceratops continued to flourish right up to the end of the Cretaceous period. It may well have been the last surviving large dinosaur in the western part of North America, and perhaps the last surviving large dinosaur in the entire world. But it, too, mysteriously died off at the end of the Cretaceous period, along with all other dinosaurs.

Hadrosaurs like Parasaurolophus spent most of their time walking on all fours looking for food.

Parasaurolophus

(pair-ah-SAW-roh-LOH-fus)
similar crested lizard
Range: *Western United States and Canada*
Length: *30 feet (9 meters)*
Weight: *4 tons (3.6 metric tons)*

T he **hadrosaurs** (HAD-row-sawrs), commonly called duck-billed dinosaurs, were one of the last large groups of dinosaurs to develop. They appeared in the middle of the Cretaceous period and evolved into a wide variety of types. They were a successful group and eventually spread throughout the northern hemisphere.

A museum exhibit shows models of a Maiasaura family.

These dinosaurs had long faces with broad, flattened, toothless snouts. That is why they are called duck-billed. Toward the back of their mouths were rows of strong teeth, hundreds of them in each jaw. New teeth continually replaced old, worn ones. This was a unique development among dinosaurs and probably accounted for the group's success. They were well adapted to eating the new and tougher plants that appeared during the Cretaceous period.

All hadrosaurs had long hind legs and shorter forelegs with hooflike nails for walking. These dinosaurs probably spent most of their time walking on all fours looking for food. When it came time to run from predators, they would have reared up on their hind legs and sprinted away. They would have used their long tails for balance.

Many hadrosaurs had bony crests on the top of their heads. These crests came in a variety of shapes and sizes. Of all the hadrosaurs, Parasaurolophus had the most striking head

Arctic Ocean

U.S.A.

Hudson
Bay

North
c Ocean

Canada

U.S.A.

Atlantic Ocean

MEXICO

Gulf
of
Mexico

Caribbean Sea

ornament. It was a backward pointing, hornlike crest mounted on the back of the skull. In some individuals the crest extended more than three feet (90 centimeters) beyond the back of the skull.

Though the crest of Parasaurolophus looks rather like a horn, it is hollow. It would have been much too fragile to be used in a fight. Besides, it is in the wrong place. The crest is so far back on the skull that it is hard to imagine how it could have been used in fighting.

What were the crests used for? Many different theories have been proposed over the years.

At one time it was believed that the hadrosaurs spent much of their time in the

Hadrosaurs such as Parasaurolophus spread through the northern hemisphere, from Mexico to Canada.

water. According to this theory, the hollow crest could have served as an underwater

A museum model shows a partial Parasaurolophus skeleton, with a wall drawing to show what the entire skeleton must have looked like.

breathing device. But scientists now believe that was not the case.

Another suggestion has been that the hollow crests provided an enlarged area for sensory

glands. As defenseless plant-eaters, hadrosaurs would have needed sharp senses. Hearing, sight, and smell would have given them warnings of the approach of predators.

But there are problems with this theory as well. If the crests held sensory glands that helped the hadrosaurs escape predators, why did the hadrosaurs with small crests, or no crests at all, survive just as well as Parasaurolophus and others with enormous crests?

The most popular theory today is that the crests were probably used as signaling devices to allow different hadrosaurs to recognize members of their own species. Most hadrosaurs are about the same size and shape. Many different hadrosaur species lived in the same area. The crests are so strikingly different that it would not have been hard to tell one from the other, even at a distance. The crests may also have been brightly colored.

Hadrosaurs apparently had excellent hearing. Parasaurolophus's hollow crest was

connected to its nose. If it breathed out strongly, the hollow crest would have helped to create a loud honking sound. Different species with different crests would have produced very different sounds. These individualized sounds would have allowed herds to keep in contact even when they could not see one another.

The late Cretaceous period might have been a very colorful and noisy time in earth's history.

Maiasaura

(my-a-SAW-ra)
good mother lizard
Range: *Western United States and Canada*
Length: *30 feet (9 meters)*
Weight: *4 tons (3.6 metric tons)*

For more than a century after dinosaurs were first discovered, scientists regarded them as little more than giant reptiles. The dinosaurs were thought to be slow moving and rather stupid. It was believed that they laid their eggs and then walked away, like most reptiles. After

A mother Maiasaura tends her nest of babies. Like some modern reptiles, the Maiasaura was protective of its young.

hatching in the heat of the sun, the young immediately had to fend for themselves.

Many of the old beliefs about dinosaurs have changed as the result of new discoveries. In 1978 a remarkable discovery in western Montana changed our view of how dinosaurs cared for their young. John Horner and Robert Makela reported finding the nesting site of a new species of hadrosaur. This new dinosaur was given the name Maiasaura, or good mother lizard.

Horner and Makela had found the remains of a complete nesting site. It was a 75 million-year-old dinosaur nursery, where this species of duck-billed dinosaur laid its eggs and where the young were able to develop and grow in safety.

Before this find, little was known about dinosaur reproduction. In the 1920s, the first dinosaur eggs were discovered in Mongolia. They belonged to Protoceratops, a small relation of the horned dinosaurs. The nests had been carefully dug in the sand. The eggs inside

them were very well preserved, considering they were 70 million years old. But this find, sensational as it was, did not tell us nearly as much about dinosaur behavior as the 1978 discovery.

What the scientists found in Montana was the skeleton of an adult dinosaur, perhaps the mother, several youngsters about three feet (90 centimeters) long, and some newly hatched

Scientists have discovered that Maiasauras carefully built nests for their eggs and their young.

dinosaurs. The hatchlings were in a nest. Nearby were several other nests with eggs and pieces of broken shell scattered around.

The nests had clearly been prepared with great care. Inside the nest, the eggs had been

laid in circles, layer upon layer. The mother probably covered each layer with sand or dirt, and then covered the whole nest the same way. This would have kept the eggs warm. It would also help conceal the eggs from marauding egg stealers.

The females nested in groups, showing that they were social animals. Evidence also shows that the dinosaurs returned to the same nesting site year after year. The young dinosaurs also stayed with their mother until they were mature enough to take care of themselves. The youngsters stayed near the nest while the mother, and perhaps the father, brought food to them.

None of this evidence should have been very surprising. Such modern reptiles as crocodiles guard their nests and their young. Birds, which may be closely related to dinosaurs, certainly do. Many birds and reptiles have communal nesting sites to which they return year after year.

The discovery of a Maiasaura nesting colony changed modern attitudes toward dinosaurs.

But in 1978 this information about Maiasaura nesting habits was surprising. At that time most people believed that dinosaurs were just too stupid to do anything as complicated as raising young. The discovery went a long way toward changing modern attitudes toward dinosaurs.

Since 1978 nesting colonies of other types of dinosaurs have been discovered. But nothing has matched the dramatic evidence found in the Maiasaura colony in Montana.

Glossary

asteroid–one of thousands of small planets or fragments of planets in our solar system

carnivorous–having the ability to eat and digest meat

Cenozoic–the era of recent life from 65 million years ago to the present

ceratopsid–a horn-faced dinosaur

comet–a body made up of frozen gas and rock that passes through our solar system

Cretaceous period–the third geological period in the Age of Dinosaurs, from 140 million to 65 million years ago

hadrosaur–a duck-billed dinosaur

herbivorous–describes a species that lives on plants and vegetation

Jurassic period–the second geological period in the Age of Dinosaurs, from 195 million to 140 million years ago

Mesozoic–the era of middle life, or the Age of Dinosaurs, from 230 million to 65 million years ago

paleontologists–scientists who study life in past ages

Paleozoic–the era of ancient life from 600 million to 230 million years ago

species–a group of animals that look the same and can breed together

Triassic period–the first geological period in the Age of Dinosaurs, from 230 million to 195 million years ago

To Learn More

Arnold, Caroline. *Dinosaur Mountain: Graveyard of the Past.* New York: Clarion Books, 1989.

Benton, Michael. *The Dinosaur Encyclopedia.* New York: Julian Messner, 1984.

Berenstain, Michael. *The Horned Dinosaur, Triceratops.* Racine, WI: Western Publishing Co., 1989.

Cohen, Daniel and Cohen, Susan. *Where to Find Dinosaurs Today.* New York: Cobblehill, 1992.

Lasky, Kathryn. *Dinosaur Dig.* New York: Morrow Junior Books, 1990.

Lauber, Patricia. *Dinosaurs Walked Here and other Stories Fossils Tell.* New York: Bradbury Press, 1991.

Lindsay, William. *The Great Dinosaur Atlas.* New York: Julian Messner, 1991.

Murphy, Jim. *The Last Dinosaur.* New York: Scholastic, 1988.

Riehecky, Janet. *Maiasaura.* Chicago: Childrens Press, 1989.

Sandell, Elizabeth J. *Maiasaura: The Good Mother Dinosaur.* Mankato, Minn: Bancroft-Sage Publications, 1988.

Steffof, Rebecca. *Extinction.* New York: Chelsea House Publishers, 1992.

Wallace, Joseph E. *The Audubon Society Pocket Guide to Dinosaurs.* New York: Knopf, 1992.

Some Useful Addresses

The Academy of Natural Sciences
19th Street and The Parkway
Philadelphia, PA 19103

The American Museum of Natural History
Central Park West at 79th Street
New York, NY 10024-5192

California Academy of Sciences
Golden Gate Park
San Francisco, CA 94118-4599

Dinosaur National Monument
P.O. Box 210
Dinosaur, CO 81610

Field Museum of Natural History
Roosevelt Road at Lake Shore Drive
Chicago, IL 60605-2496

Museum of the Rockies
South Sixth Street and Kagy Boulevard
Bozeman, MT 59717-0040

National Museum of Natural History
Smithsonian Institution
Tenth Street and Constitution Avenue N.W.
Washington, DC 20002

**Natural History Museum of Los Angeles
  County**
900 Exposition Blvd.
Los Angeles, CA 90007

New Mexico Museum of Natural History
1801 Mountain Road
Albuquerque, NM 87104

The Peabody Museum
170 Whitney Avenue
New Haven, CT 06511

Royal Ontario Museum
100 Queen's Park
Toronto, Ontario M5S 2C6
Canada

Tyrell Museum of Paleontology
Box 7500
Drumheller, Alberta T0J 0Y0
Canada

Where to View Dinosaur Tracks

Dinosaur Ridge

This is a national landmark near Morrison, west of Denver, Colorado. The hiking trail allows visitors to stroll along a trackbed from the Cretaceous period.

Dinosaur Valley State Park

This park is in Glen Rose, southwest of Fort Worth, Texas. Part of an original dinosaur trackway was excavated here. It is on view at the American Museum of Natural History in New York City.

Dinosaur State Park

Visitors to this park, in Rocky Hill, south of Hartford, Connecticut, can make plaster casts of dinosaur tracks.

For more information on dinosaur events and sites, write to:

Dinosaur Society
200 Carleton Avenue
East Islip, NY 11730
(516) 277-7855

This organization promotes research and education in the study of dinosaurs. It also publishes *Dino Times*, a monthly magazine for children. Subscriptions are $19.95 a year. *Dinosaur Report*, a quarterly magazine, costs $25 a year.

Photo credits: Linda J. Moore: p. 4; Bruce Selyem, Museum of the Rockies: pp. 8, 12, 24, 32, 35; James P. Rowan: p. 10-11; Denver Museum of Natural History: p. 20; John Weinstein, The Field Museum, Chicago IL: p. 28-29 (Neg #GEO-85859.4c); The Field Museum, Chicago, IL: p. 14 (Neg. #GEO 85828), (Neg, #59442) pp. 16-17; Museum of the Rockies: p. 36.

Index

LEADERS OF THE CIVIL WAR ERA

Frederick Douglass

LEADERS OF THE CIVIL WAR ERA

John Brown

Jefferson Davis

Frederick Douglass

Ulysses S. Grant

Stonewall Jackson

Robert E. Lee

Abraham Lincoln

William Tecumseh Sherman

Harriet Beecher Stowe

Harriet Tubman

LEADERS OF THE CIVIL WAR ERA

Frederick Douglass

Jon Sterngass

CHELSEA HOUSE
PUBLISHERS

An imprint of Infobase Publishing

J
92.
Douglass - Sterngass

FREDERICK DOUGLASS

Chelsea House
An imprint of Infobase Publishing
132 West 31st Street
New York NY 10001

Library of Congress Cataloging-in-Publication Data
Sterngass, Jon.
  Frederick Douglass / Jon Sterngass.
    p. cm. — (Leaders of the Civil War era)
  Includes bibliographical references and index.
  ISBN 978-1-60413-306-6 (hardcover : acid-free paper) 1. Douglass, Frederick, 1818-1895—Juvenile literature. 2. African American abolitionists-—Biography—Juvenile literature. 3. Abolitionists—United States—Biography—Juvenile literature. 4. Antislavery movements—United States—History—19th century—Juvenile literature. 5. Slaves—Maryland—Biography—Juvenile literature. I. Title. II. Series.
  E449.D75S74 2009
  973.8092—dc22
  [B]   2008043023

Series design by Erik Lindstrom
Cover design by Keith Trego

Printed in the United States of America

Bang FOF 10 9 8 7 6 5 4 3 2 1

This book is printed on acid-free paper.

CONTENTS

A Self-Made Man

The life of Frederick Douglass (1818–1895) spanned most of the nineteenth century. Douglass was born when slavery was universal in the American South. By the time he died, it was becoming a fading memory. Douglass was born a slave, destined for hard work and brutal treatment, with no hope and no future. Amazingly, he escaped from slavery and educated himself. Through decades of tireless efforts, he helped to free millions more.

Douglass filled many roles in his years of freedom. He was an abolitionist, a newspaper editor, a best-selling author, a lecturer, and a reformer. He is one of the most important people in American history. Throughout his life, he spoke out for the equality of all people, regardless of skin color or gender.

In an age of great speakers, Douglass was one of the best. A local newspaperman came away overwhelmed from a Douglass speech in New Hampshire. "As a speaker, he has few equals," the newspaperman said. "He has wit, argument, sarcasm, and pathos. . . . His voice is melodious and rich, and his enunciation quite elegant."

Douglass raised his voice for basic human rights. He fought just as hard to end racial discrimination in the North as he did to end slavery in the South. After the Civil War, Douglass supported constitutional amendments to guarantee voting rights and other civil rights for African Americans. He thundered against white racism and condemned white lynchings of blacks in the South.

HIS AUTOBIOGRAPHIES

Perhaps it is as an author that Douglass left his most lasting mark. His *Narrative of the Life of Frederick Douglass, An American Slave, Written by Himself* remains one of the most commonly read books in American and African-American studies. For many years, people read the *Narrative* only for its facts as those facts related to slavery. Today, Douglass is recognized as a great writer in his own right.

Douglass wrote the *Narrative* in 1845. The book is a brief and powerful declaration of freedom by a runaway slave. Written mainly as an antislavery tract, it was a bestseller at the time and remains so today.

Ten years later, Douglass wrote *My Bondage and My Freedom*. More than three times the length of the *Narrative*, *My Bondage* offers deeper reflections on slavery and the antislavery movement. *The Life and Times of Frederick Douglass*, written in 1881, is even longer than *My Bondage*. The book contains the memories of an old and famous man. He takes great pride in his honors, defends his record, and criticizes honors that he did not receive.

Frederick Douglass was one of the greatest speakers in U.S. history. Douglass became famous for his efforts to end racism and promote equality among all races. As a former slave, he managed to teach himself how to read and write and later inspired others with his articles, speeches, and books.

Despite Douglass' best efforts, however, he could not control his biography totally. That is because, in addition to his autobiographies, historians have access to thousands of his speeches, letters, and editorials. Douglass also had hundreds, if not thousands, of friends and acquaintances. Many of them voiced or wrote their own opinions of him. He befriended all types of people: female and male, black and white, American and foreign, rich and poor. Douglass was a complex human being who lived in a century and a world filled with turmoil. Yet he started his life as a piece of property in the state of Maryland.

SLAVERY AND COTTON

Before the late 1700s, Europeans wore clothes made from wool or from flax. Most people made their own clothing at home, a process that took much time and effort. The spinning and weaving of cotton were very small industries. In the late eighteenth century, major changes in agriculture, manufacturing, and transportation sparked what has come to be known as the Industrial Revolution. New machines made it easy to produce cotton cloth cheaply and in large amounts. Soon, there was a tremendous demand for cotton to feed the new machines. The Industrial Revolution, which began in Great Britain, spread throughout Europe, North America, and, eventually, the world.

In 1790, the entire United States produced only 3,000 bales of cotton. Cotton grew well in many areas of the South, but one big problem stood between the growers and an increase in production. The seeds were so difficult to remove from the cotton fiber that it took an entire day for one person to hand-clean a single pound of cotton. In the 1790s, a number of inventors, including Eli Whitney, developed a machine to separate the seeds from the fiber of cotton. The cotton gin (short for "engine") was simply a hand-cranked cylinder with metal teeth. Now it was possible for someone to clean 50 pounds of cotton a day.

After the invention of the cotton gin in the 1700s, people flocked to the South hoping to make money by starting a cotton plantation. By using black slave workers, plantation owners were able to increase cotton production for a larger profit. Above, an African-American man works a cotton gin in South Carolina.

As the United States expanded, so did the farming of cotton. Thousands of white settlers moved into the interior of South Carolina and Georgia to grow cotton. The growers used black slaves as workers. By 1811, this area produced 60 million pounds of cotton per year. Soon, white farmers rushed into Alabama and Mississippi with their black slaves. By 1860, the southern United States grew 60 percent of the world's cotton.

AMERICAN COTTON PRODUCTION

YEAR	BALES OF U.S. COTTON
1800	73,000
1820	335,000
1840	1,348,000
1859	4,508,000

The number of slaves grew tremendously. In 1860, about one-third of all Southern white families owned slaves. Many other Southerners hoped to own slaves. Powerful slave owners dominated politics, the courts, and sheriffs' offices in the South. At the same time, in the North, because of climate and economy, slavery failed to develop on such a scale as it had in the South. Eventually, in the North, slavery died out.

MISERY FOR AFRICAN AMERICANS

Growing cotton meant opportunity for white planters. It did not mean opportunity for slaves. To slaves, cotton meant misery. Whites uprooted thousands of African Americans from the Chesapeake or Carolina regions of the East Coast and forced them to move west. Slave families were separated, and children were sold away from their parents. About one out of every four African-American families was broken up because of the slave trade. By 1860, almost one million American slaves had been moved against their will from the place of their birth to the booming cotton states.

Enslaved blacks on cotton plantations often worked from dawn to dusk, and sometimes even longer. Slaves cleared the land, tended the crops, and built the houses. Household slaves cooked, cleaned, and took care of the master's children. Enslaved African Americans were not paid for their work.

Their labor and their lives literally were stolen by their white masters. Slave women had to endure sexual abuse and rape. They often bore the children of their masters and overseers. Masters disciplined slaves by whipping, imprisonment, torture, and mutilation. Southern laws considered enslaved human beings to be, quite simply and strictly, property. In the early 1800s, this was life for one out of every seven people in the "free republic" of the United States.

Life for free blacks was not much better. In most of the South, free African Americans enjoyed none of the civil rights that were set forth in the Bill of Rights. A free black American could not vote or testify against a white person in court. Even in the North, the rights of free blacks were severely restricted.

NO STRUGGLE, NO PROGRESS

Douglass was born into this system of slavery. Through remarkable determination and intelligence, he managed to rise from the despair of slavery to become an adviser to presidents. Despite all the difficulties of his life, he remained optimistic to the end. Looking back, Douglass commented that his life "has at times been dark and stormy, and I have met with hardships from which other men have been exempted, yet my life has in many respects been remarkably full of sunshine and joy."

AFRICAN AMERICANS IN THE UNITED STATES

YEAR	NORTH FREE	NORTH SLAVE	SOUTH FREE	SOUTH SLAVE
1800	47,000	37,000	61,000	857,000
1820	99,000	19,000	34,000	1,519,000
1840	171,000	1,000	16,000	2,486,000
1850	226,000	—	262,000	3,954,000

Douglass often noted that his mother was black, but his father was white. He was 100 percent American, with family roots on both sides, which probably stretched back for generations. "I am an American citizen," Douglass thundered. "In birth, in sentiment, in ideas, in hopes, in aspirations, and responsibilities, I am an American citizen."

Douglass often was denied his rights as an American. Despite racism and prejudice, however, he never lost his pride in himself. Throughout his life, Douglass fought for the rights not only of African Americans, but also of all Americans, to be equal parts of the national family. Douglass knew that this would not come easily. "If there is no struggle . . . there is no progress," he said. "Power concedes nothing without a demand. It never did and it never will."

"I Was Born in Tuckahoe"

"I was born in Tuckahoe, near Hillsborough, and about twelve miles from Easton, in Talbot County, Maryland." So begins Frederick Douglass' famous narrative of his childhood as a slave and of his escape to the North as a young man. The statement sounds very simple, but, in fact, it carries special meaning.

Douglass was born a slave. By Maryland law, he was a thing, a piece of property with no historic identity. A white person of Douglass' time who wrote an autobiography would have taken it for granted that he or she had a name, a birth date, a place of birth, and a home. For a slave, who could be bought or sold at any time, it was different. When Douglass wanted to tell the story of his life, he first had to show that he existed as a person. By beginning his *Narrative* with the words "I was born," Douglass attached himself to a place and to a society. He was not simply a piece of property like a table or a barn. He was a person. He existed.

Douglass was born in February 1818. His mother named him Frederick Augustus Washington Bailey. His first home was a lonely cabin in the woods on the Eastern Shore of Maryland. The Eastern Shore was a long peninsula between the Atlantic Ocean and Chesapeake Bay. Young Frederick lived with his maternal grandmother, Betsy Bailey. Betsy was a slave, and her children and grandchildren all were slaves.

Frederick's mother was named Harriet Bailey. Unfortunately, he had almost no memory of her. She lived on a plantation about 12 miles away from the cabin. He later could recall only about five visits that she made, at night, to the cabin. "I cannot say I was deeply attached to my mother," Douglass wrote in his book. "I never think of this terrible interference of slavery with my infantile affections and its diverting them from their natural course, without feelings to which I can give no adequate expression." When Frederick was about seven, he heard that his mother had died from a long illness. He remembered receiving "the tidings of her death with much the same emotions I should have probably felt at the death of a stranger." She had died without telling him, or probably anyone else, who his father was.

It always frustrated Douglass not to know his father's identity. He wrote, "My father was a white man. He was admitted to be such by all I ever heard speak of my parentage." Perhaps his master, Aaron Anthony, was his father. Anthony lived a dozen miles away at Wye House, the estate near Chesapeake Bay that he managed for the Edward Lloyd family. Frederick never would know for sure, however.

Douglass' black and white ancestors probably had lived on the Eastern Shore of Maryland for more than a century. The black Baileys, although slaves, were a strong family. The Baileys had deep roots in the area and a long tradition of courage and endurance. The name "Bailey" had been passed down for five straight generations of black women under various spellings.

"The last time Fred saw his mother."

Born as a slave, Frederick Douglass was raised by his grandmother. Knowing only that his father was white, Douglass grew up with a lack of identity and a sense of abandonment. He continued to struggle with these feelings throughout his life and wrote about them in his autobiography. Left, an illustration of the last time Douglass saw his mother from his autobiography, *Narrative of the Life of Frederick Douglass, An American Slave, Written by Himself*.

Betsy Bailey was intelligent and physically powerful. She was expert in fishing, farming, and putting food on the table. Frederick's childhood in her cabin was very happy. He wrote that he was, "for the most part . . . a spirited, joyous, uproarious, and happy boy, upon whom troubles fall only like water on a duck's back." Years later, Douglass remembered his childhood as the golden period of his life. "Even in the gloomiest days of [Maryland's] history, and my own, I have felt an inexpressible affection for my native state," Douglass told a Baltimore crowd in 1864. "Eastern Shore corn and Eastern Shore pork gave me my muscle," he said. "I love Maryland and the Eastern Shore!"

Betsy took care of all the infants in the Bailey family. That allowed their mothers (her daughters) to work on Anthony's farms. When Betsy's grandchildren were old enough to help, they were called to work at Wye House. In 1824, when Frederick was six, his grandmother brought him to Wye House. His older brother and sisters—Perry, Sarah, and Eliza— already had made this move. After bringing him to Wye House, Frederick's grandmother left quietly, without telling the child. When Frederick found out, he felt crushed. "I had never been deceived before," he remembered, 50 years later, "and something of resentment mingled with my grief at parting with my grandmother." He never fully trusted anyone again.

"THE BLOOD-STAINED GATE"

Edward Lloyd V, the owner of Wye House, was one of the richest men in Maryland. He loved to show off his possessions. Half a

THE SEARCH FOR A BIRTHDAY

For his entire life, Frederick Douglass was obsessed with who he was, when he was born, and where he came from. "I have no accurate knowledge of my age, never having seen any authentic record containing it," Douglass wrote in the *Narrative*. "By far the larger part of the slaves know as little of their ages as horses know of theirs, and it is the wish of most masters within my knowledge to keep their slaves thus ignorant. I do not remember to have ever met a slave who could tell his birthday."

It annoyed young Frederick that white children could tell their ages and he could not. The institution of slavery turned people into things. It denied them a birth date, a name, a family structure, and legal rights.

The question of Douglass' background haunted him throughout his adulthood. Douglass kept searching, with no reward, to discover the identity of his father. He often

century later, Douglass remembered, "Immense wealth and its lavish expenditure, fill the great house with all that can please the eye, or tempt the taste." The Lloyds had lived like English lords on the Eastern Shore since the 1660s.

Edward Lloyd V was a former governor of Maryland and a U.S. senator. He owned at least 13 farms, more than 10,000 acres, and several hundred slaves. The Lloyd family fortune had been built on tobacco, but the last Lloyd tobacco crop was planted in 1825. Edward Lloyd replaced it with wheat and became the biggest wheat farmer in Maryland. The handsome Wye House, built in the 1780s, was entirely self-sufficient. Only the many luxuries had to be imported.

felt torn between the races, troubled by being both black and white and yet neither. "Slavery made my brothers and sisters strangers to me," Douglass wrote. "It converted the mother that bore me into a myth; it shrouded my father in mystery, and left me without an intelligible beginning in the world."

Douglass had more luck with his birth year. Working from slender clues, he concluded that he probably was born in 1817. He was not absolutely sure that this year was correct, however. Despite the uncertainty, on his tombstone, the inscription reads "1817-1895."

As it turned out, there was a written record of his birth. In the late 1900s, a historian discovered ledgers kept by Douglass' master, Aaron Anthony. These books contain a table entitled "My Black People," with the notation *"Frederick Augustus son of Harriet Feby 1818."* This date also agrees with other external evidence, and it is now certain that Douglass' birth year was 1818.

The Lloyd family built its fortune on the backs of slave labor. Local people knew the family as cruel owners who gave their slaves the minimum of food, clothing, and shelter. The Lloyds seldom sold slaves and never freed them. Few plantations provided a bigger contrast between the riches of the great house and the poverty of the slave quarters only a few hundred yards away.

Aaron Anthony was Edward Lloyd's chief lieutenant and perhaps Frederick's father. Douglass later described Anthony as a mean old man on the edge of mental illness. When Anthony was younger, however, he rose from poverty to be the main overseer of Lloyd's estate. By the time of his death, Anthony was a moderately wealthy planter in his own right: He owned 3 farms that totaled 600 acres and 30 slaves.

At the time of Douglass' childhood, there were about 80 black children on Edward Lloyd's central farm. Young Frederick was chosen ahead of many other eligible slaves to be the personal companion of 12-year-old Daniel Lloyd, Edward's youngest son. Considering the circumstances, it is clear that, even at age six, Frederick was recognized by his white masters as an exceptional child. For a slave, he lived a charmed life at the Wye House. He later said, "I have nothing cruel or shocking to relate of my own personal experience while I remained on Col. Lloyd's plantation."

Young Frederick was lucky. Rule by terror was common on Lloyd's plantation. Whipping was a usual punishment. Later, Douglass remembered several cruel overseers who seemed to enjoy whipping slaves. He cited many examples of whippings that he saw personally, as well as others that he had heard about. He even gave accounts of overseers who murdered their slaves and went unpunished. Many of the descriptions in Douglass' memoirs emphasized brutal attacks by white male masters on slave women.

Young Frederick slowly learned that he was a slave. His introduction into the reality of being owned by someone else was particularly terrifying. Early one morning, six-year-old Frederick heard screams in the kitchen. As he cowered on the floor of the little closet where he slept, Frederick could see his young aunt Esther (who worked in the kitchen) with her wrists firmly tied and the rope fastened to a heavy wooden beam. A white man was whipping Frederick's aunt on "her naked back till she was literally covered with blood." Frederick remembered with horror that, "No words, no tears, no prayers, from his gory victim, seemed to move his iron heart from its bloody purpose. The louder she screamed, the harder he whipped; and where the blood ran fastest, there he whipped longest."

Douglass never forgot the scene. He recalled it in detail in all his autobiographies. He called it "the blood-stained gate, the entrance to the hell of slavery, through which I was about to pass. It was a most terrible spectacle." This looked as if it would be his fate: to be whipped at someone else's pleasure.

Slaves lived in fear of being whipped or killed, but the alternative was possibly even worse. Maryland slaves in the days of Douglass' youth dreaded being "sold down to Georgia." This fate meant that they would end their lives on the fields of a cotton plantation, far from their families, friends, and native soil. The terrible threat of sale to the Deep South haunted young Frederick's dreams. Later, in Baltimore, it gave him nightmares and inspired his escape.

FELL'S POINT

In 1826, Aaron Anthony allowed Frederick to go to Baltimore to live with Hugh Auld, the brother of Anthony's son-in-law, Thomas Auld. "I shall never forget the ecstasy with which I received the intelligence that my old master (Anthony) had determined to let me go to Baltimore," Douglass remembered. "I received this information about three days before my departure. They were three of the happiest days I ever enjoyed." Frederick had been at Wye House for 18 months; he would not return for 55 years. He called his removal from the Lloyds' plantation "one of the most . . . fortunate events of my life." In Baltimore, Frederick Bailey had a different home and a different way of life.

How different, Frederick realized when the front door first opened. "I saw what I had never seen before; it was a white face beaming with the most kindly emotions," Frederick marveled. "It was the face of my new mistress, Sophia Auld." As time passed, and despite many difficulties in their relationship, Frederick came to regard Sophia "as something more akin to a mother than a slaveholding mistress." Technically, Frederick was supposed to take care of Tommy, the Auld's two-year-old son. In truth, Frederick had very few responsibilities beyond running the occasional errand. He spent a good deal of time roaming through the growing port of Baltimore.

The Aulds lived in the Fell's Point area of Baltimore. This hooked piece of land that jutted out on the east side of the outer harbor was the city's busy shipbuilding center. Shipyards and docks lined the Fell's Point waterfront. From Baltimore's wharves, merchants exported wheat, flour, and tobacco to Europe. The ships returned with luxury items, such as coffee from Brazil.

Baltimore also was a leading port of entry for Irish and German immigrants. Many of them stayed to work in the shipyards and on the docks. It was a stimulating environment for a brilliant and curious child. "Going to live at Baltimore," Frederick said, "laid the foundation, and opened the gateway, to all my subsequent prosperity."

RANKED WITH HORSES, SHEEP, AND SWINE

Young Frederick spent more than a year in the calm Auld household, until Aaron Anthony died in November 1826. In the aftermath of Anthony's death, Frederick was swiftly reminded that a slave's life was not his own to control. Because Anthony died without a will, his property had to be valued and divided among his heirs. In October 1827, a group of lawyers assembled to value and distribute all of Anthony's slaves as part of the settlement. Frederick was shipped to the Tuckahoe farm.

Douglass later remembered with bitterness, "We were all ranked together at the valuation. Men and women, old and young, married and single, were ranked with horses, sheep, and swine." In a flash, Frederick understood that slaves were just things to be assigned a price and sold at market. "At this moment," Douglass recalled, "I saw more clearly than ever the brutalizing effects of slavery upon both slave and slaveholder." Twenty-eight slaves, including the eight-year-old Frederick, were valued, in total, at $2,805.

Anthony's heirs were his three children: Andrew, Richard, and Lucretia. In 1823, Lucretia had met and married ship-builder Thomas Auld (1795–1880), a man who had been living as a boarder in the Anthony home. After Lucretia's death, in the summer of 1827, her share of her father's estate fell to her husband.

The lawyers settled the Anthony estate by dividing the slaves into three equal valuations, according to slave family groupings. Frederick was the main exception. He was given to Thomas Auld, who almost certainly had specifically requested him. In doing this, Auld saved young Frederick from a life with Auld's drunken and cruel brothers-in-law. Thomas then helped Frederick again by promptly sending him back to Sophia and Hugh Auld in Baltimore. It was not the last time that Thomas did young Frederick a favor.

LEARNING TO READ

For almost six years, Frederick lived with Hugh and Sophia in Baltimore. In Fell's Point, he was the light-skinned slave boy who lived with a family that had no other slaves. He lived in a household that gave him security and in a neighborhood that gave him stimulation. Sophia read the Bible with her son Tommy on her knee and Frederick sitting next to her.

When Frederick was about 12, Sophia began to teach him the alphabet. Although Maryland had no laws forbidding teach-

SLAVERY IN MARYLAND

The Eastern Shore of Maryland is a relative backwater today. In the 1700s, however, it was the most prosperous and thickly settled area of colonial Maryland. Slavery developed on the Eastern Shore tobacco farms and plantations in the mid-1700s. In the late 1700s, when tobacco production declined, farmers began to grow wheat instead. Tobacco represented 90 percent of Maryland's total agricultural production in 1747 but only 14 percent in 1859. The Eastern Shore began to stagnate. Census figures show that in 1790, there were 13,084 people in the Eastern Shore's Talbot County. Sixty years later, in 1850, there were only 700 more.

The decline of tobacco made slaves less valuable in Maryland. Growing tobacco could keep a slave force busy throughout the year. Wheat, on the other hand, required many workers at harvesttime but offered no work for large crews at other times. When wheat became the main crop, many Maryland farmers decreased their slave holdings. Between 1810 and 1850, Maryland's slave population declined by almost 20 percent, and the slave population of the Eastern Shore declined by 33 percent. Slaves were nearly one-third of Maryland's population in 1790 but less than one-sixth in 1850.

Some Maryland masters manumitted (freed) their slaves. More than half the blacks who lived in Maryland in 1830 were free. Talbot County, where Douglass was born,

ing slaves to read, it went against common custom. When Sophia told her husband about it, he strongly disapproved. "Learning would spoil the best nigger in the world," he said. "If you teach that nigger how to read, there would be no keeping him. It would

had one of the largest populations of free blacks of any Maryland county. Even as a child, Douglass dismissed the claim that God had commanded the enslavement of dark-skinned people. He personally knew many black people who were not slaves.

Other Maryland masters sold their slaves to buyers in the booming cotton belt of the Deep South. Before the 1820s, owners in Maryland rarely sold slaves. Instead, the slaves were handed down from generation to generation. The changing Maryland economy of the nineteenth century led landowners to sell off slaves, however. Between 1830 and 1840, nearly 12 percent of the total slave population of Maryland ended up on the auction block. In Talbot County, the number was 14 percent.

Douglass' maternal family, the Baileys, had lived on the Eastern Shore for more than 100 years. In the century before his birth, no member of Douglass' family had ever been sold away from the Eastern Shore. Yet, in the first 14 years of Douglass' life, his sister, two aunts, seven first cousins, and at least five other near relatives disappeared without a trace into the Deep South. In 1825, Talbot County slave owners received more than $20,000 from one slave-trading company alone for sales of slaves. Betsy Bailey, Douglass' grandmother, died in 1849. By the time of her death, nine of her children, grandchildren, and great grandchildren had been sold south, never to be seen by her again.

Frederick Douglass lived with the family of Sophia Auld, a kind woman who introduced the alphabet to Douglass *(depicted above)*. Life in Baltimore with the Aulds allowed Douglass to think and learn, and he was soon exposed to abolitionist ideas. He would later say, "Going to live at Baltimore laid the foundation, and opened the gateway, to all my subsequent prosperity."

forever unfit him to be a slave. He would at once become unmanageable. . . . As to himself, it could do him no good, but a great deal of harm. It would make him discontented and unhappy."

Douglass later called Hugh's response the "first decidedly anti-slavery lecture" he had ever heard. From that moment on, young Frederick believed that learning was "the pathway from slavery to freedom." If knowledge made a person unfit to be a slave, then knowledge was what Frederick wanted. Even though Sophia stopped teaching him, Frederick succeeded in learning to read with help from white children in the Fell's Point neighborhood. He then learned to write by watching the writings of men with whom he sometimes worked in a Baltimore shipyard.

As Frederick learned to read, he began to look for whatever newspapers or books that he could find. At about age 12, he discovered *The Columbian Orator* by Caleb Bingham. "Every opportunity I got, I used to read this book," Douglass later remembered. The book was a collection of political essays, poems, and dialogues, first published in 1797. It was widely used in American schoolrooms in the early 1800s. It gave examples of speeches for students to copy and imitate. Many of these speeches, such as ones by George Washington, the Greek philosopher Socrates, and the Roman statesman Cicero, celebrated patriotism, democracy, education, and freedom.

Young Frederick Bailey practiced the speeches in the books for hours. He especially liked the examples of dialogues between a master and a slave. Caleb Bingham had been a critic of slavery and included several antislavery pieces in his book. Reading them, Frederick understood that slavery was not his inevitable and natural position. "The more I read, the more I was led to abhor and detest my enslavers," Douglass recalled. They were just "a band of successful robbers, who had left their homes, gone to Africa, and stolen us from our homes, and in a strange land reduced us to slavery." He would later credit *The Columbian Orator* with helping him to explain in words why slavery was wrong. He so loved the book that he carried it with him when he escaped from slavery in 1838.

At first, learning to read and write did not help Frederick. In fact, it had the opposite effect. "As I read, behold! The very discontent so graphically predicted by Master Hugh had already come upon me," he wrote. "I was no longer the lighthearted, gleesome boy, full of mirth and play that I was when I landed in Baltimore. . . . In moments of agony, I envied my fellow-slaves for their stupidity. I . . . found myself regretting my own existence, and wished myself dead."

In the end, however, Frederick's ability to read and write did help him. His desperate desire to learn gave him the weapons to fight the oppression of slavery.

How a Slave Was Made a Man

In March 1833, Frederick Bailey left Baltimore and returned to Thomas Auld, who lived in St. Michaels, Maryland. The reason for the change is unclear. It may have been caused by a family argument between Hugh and Thomas. Frederick was 15 years old now. He was in rebellion against everything in his world. He did not get along with Thomas's new wife, Rowena Hambleton, whom Auld had married in 1829. He despised the sleepy, rundown port of St. Michaels, which was so unlike Baltimore. He longed to escape from slavery, and he openly defied Auld. After nine months, Auld realized that the sullen, strong teenage slave was not going to be useful in town.

Auld decided to hire Frederick out in January 1834 to Edward Covey. Covey was an ambitious man who rented a farm about seven miles from St. Michaels. Covey was hard-working, but he also was cruel and sly. Covey, Douglass noted, "had acquired a very high reputation for breaking young slaves." Local farmers sent Covey their slaves to use for free. He returned them to their owners "broken in." He was known to use the whip often on his slaves.

Frederick worked for Covey for a year. It was the city boy's first experience as a field slave. For six months, Covey regularly beat Frederick with sticks or cow skins. (Cow skins were leather whips that hurt the victim more because they did not break.) He forced Frederick to work from sunup to past sundown. Covey barely gave the slaves time to eat their meals.

In later years, Douglass showed off the scars on his back. They proved that he had suffered under slavery and gave him the authority to speak out. In the summer of 1834, however, he was just another slave who had been whipped and could do nothing about it. "I was somewhat unmanageable when I first went there," Douglass later wrote, "but a few months of this discipline tamed me. I was broken in body, soul, and spirit . . . the dark night of slavery closed in upon me; and behold a man transformed into a brute!"

Covey's farm was close to beautiful Chesapeake Bay. Sometimes, Frederick looked out and saw the white sails of boats against the blue water of the bay. In one of the most eloquent passages from his *Narrative*, Douglass remembered thinking,

> You are loosed from your moorings, and are free. I am fast in my chains, and am a slave! You move merrily before the gentle gale, and I sadly before the bloody whip! . . . O, that I were on one of your gallant decks, and under your protecting wing! Alas! betwixt me and you, the turbid waters roll. Go on, go on. O, that I could also go! Could I but swim! If I could fly! O, why was I born a man, of whom to make a

brute! The glad ship is gone; she hides in the dim distance. I am left in the hottest hell of unending slavery. . . . Is there any God? Why am I a slave? I will run away. I will not stand it. Get caught, or get clear, I'll try it. . . . I have only one life to lose. I had as well be killed running as die standing. Only think of it; one hundred miles north, and I am free! Try it? Yes! God helping me, I will. It cannot be that I shall live and die a slave.

THE FIGHT WITH EDWARD COVEY

In August 1834, Frederick was working in the fields, separating wheat grain from chaff, when he collapsed from sunstroke. Covey kicked him and slashed his head with a hickory stick. Frederick was outraged. When he recovered, he decided to run away and tell Thomas Auld how he was being treated. When Frederick got to St. Michaels, Auld offered him no sympathy. Instead, Auld told the bleeding Frederick to go back to Covey.

When Frederick returned, Covey tried to whip him again. What followed forms one of the most famous scenes in the history of American slavery. "You have seen how a man was made a slave," Douglass later wrote, "you shall see how a slave was made a man." What happened was that, in Douglass' words, "at this moment—from whence came the spirit I don't know—I resolved to fight."

In each written retelling of the story, Douglass kept expanding the scene. In the *Narrative*, the story occupies about 13 pages of one chapter. Ten years later, in *My Bondage and My Freedom*, the tale takes up nearly 26 pages of 3 chapters. Douglass never could explain, however, why he finally decided to resist.

The slave and the overseer wrestled furiously for nearly two hours. Douglass portrayed this fight as an epic battle between good and evil. Covey "asked me if I meant to persist in my resistance," he recalled. "I told him I did, come what might;

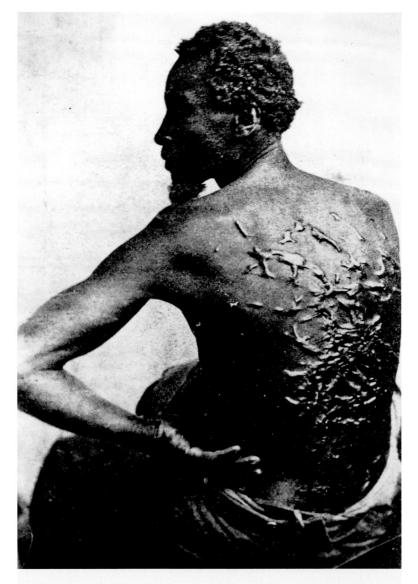

Slave owners and overseers would commonly punish their slaves by savagely whipping or beating them, often leaving horrific scars, like on the slave above. Once removed from the Auld household, Frederick Douglass received similar scars as he was ruled over by a notorious farmer known for being cruel to slaves. Routinely beaten and barely fed, Douglass toiled in the fields and temporarily lost his rebellious spirit.

that he had used me like a brute for six months, and that I was determined to be used so no longer."

A key element of the story occurs when Covey calls on two slaves to help him. Both slaves either pretend to misunderstand Covey or refuse to help him. One tells him, "My master hired me here, to work, and not to help you whip Frederick." In this way, Frederick's fellow slaves find a way to side with him and aid his resistance.

The fight ended with Covey giving up the contest. Douglass later wrote that "he had not whipped me at all. He had not drawn a single drop of blood from me. I had drawn blood from him." Frederick never was punished for his insolence. It may have been because of Covey's embarrassment or perhaps because of Thomas Auld's intercession. Frederick's last six months with Covey passed without any whippings at all.

Douglass later described the scene of the struggle with Covey as "a glorious resurrection from the tomb of slavery, to the heaven of freedom." The fight reversed his earlier entry through the "blood-stained gate of slavery." The battle with Covey formed the centerpiece of the *Narrative*. It was "the turning point of my career as a slave," Douglass said. "It rekindled the few expiring embers of freedom, and revived within me a sense of my own manhood. I might remain a slave in form, the day had passed forever when I could be a slave in fact." After the battle with Covey, Douglass never again identified himself as a brute.

Readers of the *Narrative* always hope that Covey, the symbol of evil, suffered for his crimes and ended his life in poverty and disgrace. The opposite is true. Covey advanced from his status as a poor rent farmer to owning $23,000 in real estate and five slaves by 1850. When he died, in 1875, his estate came to more than $15,000 even though he had given away most of his property to his children. To the end of his life, Covey never disputed Douglass' version of the fight or told his own.

FAILED ESCAPE

After the failure of Frederick's service with Covey, Thomas Auld tried a different strategy with his rebellious slave. Auld hired Frederick out to William Freeland for the year of 1835. Freeland was a lenient master who almost never used the whip. Douglass wrote, "My treatment, while in his employment, was heavenly, compared with what I experienced at the hands of Mr. Edward Covey."

Frederick was now 17. He worked in the fields with other young black men. Frederick and his four closest friends began to plan an escape. They hoped to steal a big oyster-gathering canoe, make their way up the Eastern Shore, and slip into Pennsylvania, a free state. Frederick wrote the counterfeit freedom passes that the four men needed to prove that they were free blacks and therefore allowed to travel. The young men decided to leave on April 2, 1836. Someone, however, betrayed their plans. Before they could make their escape, an armed posse captured Frederick and the others.

The posse forced the five slaves to walk from Freeland Farm to St. Michaels. People lined the streets to watch them come into town. Many onlookers called out that Frederick should be hanged or burned. Lynching—being put to death by a mob—was a very real possibility. Torture, or even death, was the usual punishment for a slave involved in a supposed slave insurrection. Even without evidence, no one doubted that the young men had planned an escape and that Frederick was the ringleader.

Once again, Thomas Auld interfered with the customary rules. Auld insisted that, because no one had been killed, lynching was not justified. Auld also insisted on a trial. The five tied-up slaves now had to walk for 15 miles to Easton, Maryland, where they were jailed. Frederick faced a possible sale to the endless labor of the brutal cotton fields of the Deep South. Such a sale was the typical solution for a slave caught plotting an escape from Maryland.

Auld had a problem. His slave was known to be dangerous. If Frederick escaped, Auld would get no money for him. If Frederick stayed, he probably would get into more trouble and end up dead. The obvious answer, for Auld, was to sell his slave south. After a night spent walking the floor, however, Auld decided that no amount of money could tempt him to sell Frederick to the Deep South. As Frederick Douglass' biographer wrote, "Whatever the tortured bond between the two, whether kinship or some equally strong tie, Auld could not doom the boy, now grown to be a man—a person—about whom in his clumsy, tormented way he cared immensely."

After a week, Auld had Frederick released from jail. He told his neighbors that he was going to sell Frederick to Alabama. Instead, Auld sent him back to his brother Hugh in Baltimore. Auld probably suspected that the bright young man either would get into fatal trouble in Baltimore or would escape to the North. Either way, Auld would lose Frederick. Auld put him on a boat for Fell's Point, saying that if Frederick behaved himself properly, Auld would emancipate him when he turned 25. The two did not meet again for 41 years.

HIRING OUT IN BALTIMORE

Frederick could not believe his good fortune. "After three years spent in the country, roughing it in the field . . . I was again permitted to return to Baltimore, the very place of all others, short of a free-state, where I most desired to live." Frederick moved in with Hugh and Sophia Auld again. Things were different now, however. Frederick was 18, powerfully built, and well over six feet tall. He had worked in the fields for two years and had been sent to jail. Little Tommy also was grown up. As Douglass noted, "He could grow, and become a MAN; I could grow, though I could not become a man, but must remain, all my life, a minor—a mere boy."

After his failed escape attempt, Douglass was sent to Baltimore *(above)* with the promise of emancipation when he turned 25. Though he was able to find work in Baltimore's shipyard on his own, Douglass was still required to pay Hugh Auld, his master, a certain amount of money every week. The experience gave Douglass his first taste of freedom, as he was allowed to live independently, away from his owners.

Frederick still loved living in Baltimore, however. Hugh arranged for Frederick to serve as an apprentice caulker in a shipyard. (A caulker seals the seams in wooden boats or ships, often with hot tar, to make the seams watertight.) There was plenty of work for caulkers in the city. By the 1830s, the fast-growing port of Baltimore rivaled Philadelphia and New York City. Some of Frederick's later memories of Baltimore in this period were warmly nostalgic. He recalled the "pungent fragrance of the boiling pitch," the look of "the seams of a ship's deck," the "ringing, cheerful sounds of a caulker's mallet," and hundreds of men pouring through the Fell's Point streets when a tolling bell indicated a change in shifts.

Thousands of former slaves and descendants of slaves lived in the city. They worked on the docks and in domestic service in houses and hotels. Frederick noticed that "a city slave is almost a freeman, compared with a slave on the plantation. He is much better fed and clothed, and enjoys privileges altogether unknown to the slave on the plantation."

Slavery declined in most Southern cities after 1820. Slave labor simply did not seem to work in an urban setting. Slaves could work in a city just as easily as on a plantation. City life weakened slave discipline, however. The problem in cities was not to find work for slaves, but to control them when their work was finished. As Douglass later noted, "Slavery dislikes a dense population, in which there is a majority of non-slaveholders."

In the spring of 1838, Frederick made a deal with Hugh Auld. Auld granted Frederick the privilege of hiring himself out in Baltimore. Frederick would schedule his own time, find work, bargain for wages, and purchase his own tools, food, and clothing. In exchange, he would pay Auld three dollars a week. "Master Hugh seemed to be very much pleased . . . with this arrangement," Douglass noted, "and well he might be for it was decidedly in his favor. . . . While he derived all of the benefits of slaveholding . . . without its evils, I endured all the evils of being a slave and yet suffered all the care and anxiety of a responsible freeman."

Frederick's situation was not unique. In Southern cities, masters commonly hired out their slaves to other employers for specific periods of time. Baltimore's economy was extremely uneven. It depended on the season, the weather, and the trade cycles. The slave system did not meet these irregular demands. Hiring out gave slave owners some flexibility.

Slaves also liked the hiring-out system. It gave them undreamed of independence. Frederick eagerly moved out of the Fell's Point house into his own place. This was the first time in his life that he lived independently of a master. From May to August, he went on a feverish quest for money. "In the enjoyment of excellent health," he noted, he "was ready to work by

BLACKS IN BALTIMORE POPULATION, 1810–1840

YEAR	TOTAL POP.	TOTAL SLAVES	% OF SLAVES	TOTAL FREE BLACKS	% OF FREE BLACKS	TOTAL BLACK POP.	% TOTAL BLACKS
1810	46,555	4,672	10.0%	5,671	12.2%	10,243	22.0%
1820	62,738	4,357	6.9%	10,326	16.5%	14,683	23.4%
1830	70,620	4,120	5.8%	14,790	20.1%	18,910	26.8%
1840	102,513	3,212	3.1%	17,980	17.5%	21,192	20.7%

Source: Barbara Jeanne Fields, Slavery and Freedom on the Middle Ground: Maryland during the Nineteenth Century. New Haven: Yale University Press, 1985, p. 62.

night as by day." Frederick knew that some slaves made enough money by hiring out to purchase their own freedom.

Hiring out also had its drawbacks. Slaves often had to deal with the hostility of white workers who were doing the same jobs. Frederick experienced verbal and physical abuse from white apprentices in shipyards. They saw blacks, slave and free, as competitors who were undercutting their wages.

ANNA MURRAY AND THE FREE BLACKS OF BALTIMORE

Living without a white master, Frederick soon found a black peer group. He associated with a group of free black caulkers in Fell's Point known as the East Baltimore Mental Improvement Society. In this organization, blacks discussed the major political issues of the day. Despite its serious name, the society also served as a site for social gatherings.

It was not unusual for Frederick Bailey, as a skilled urban worker, to be working alongside free blacks even though he was a slave. In Maryland, by the eve of the Civil War, free black people were nearly as numerous as enslaved black people. No other slave state (except Delaware) approached Maryland in either the absolute or relative size of its free black population. The number of free black people in Baltimore, Maryland, rose by 3,000 percent from 1800 to 1850. In 1850, Baltimore claimed 17 percent of Maryland's black population but 34 percent of the state's free black population. The growth of Maryland's free black population meant that free blacks inevitably came into close contact with slaves.

Free blacks were free to leave the state. Bonds of marriage, family, and friendship kept them in Maryland, however. Free blacks tried desperately to carve out a small space for themselves in an extremely hostile and suspicious white world. Free black people in Maryland were not allowed to own dogs or firearms, or to purchase liquor or ammunition without a special license.

In Baltimore, free blacks created their own subculture. They had their own churches, clubs, schools, and informal gathering places that were unconnected to the white world. The busy seaport provided work for unskilled laborers, servants, grain measurers, dock and warehouse workers, coal-handlers, and carters. Free blacks in Baltimore also held craft positions as carpenters, blacksmiths, barbers, and caulkers.

This was the world of Anna Murray. She was a free black woman who was working in domestic service in Baltimore. Murray was born, probably in 1813, on the Eastern Shore. She was the eighth child of slaves who had been freed just before her birth. At 17, she moved to Baltimore and worked as a domestic worker. She apparently met Douglass at meetings of the East Baltimore Mental Improvement Society. Because Douglass wrote very little about Anna, it is not clear how they met or what she was like. In 1838, two years after they met, Frederick and Anna were married in New York City.

ESCAPE FROM SLAVERY

One Saturday, late in the summer of 1838, Frederick went to a meeting outside Baltimore. He had such a good time that he stayed away from the city for an extra day. He had not paid Hugh Auld his weekly wage before he left for the meeting. Frederick had grown cocky. He thought that he could pay

RATIO OF FREE BLACKS TO SLAVES IN MARYLAND, 1790–1850

YEAR	RATIO
1790	.08
1810	.30
1830	.51
1850	.83

Source: Barbara Jeanne Fields, Slavery and Freedom on the Middle Ground: Maryland during the Nineteenth Century. New Haven: Yale University Press, 1985, p. 2.

his master a day or so late. Auld was furious when Frederick returned, two days late. Auld ordered his slave to give up his independent employment and housing and move back to Auld's house, where his master could keep an eye on him.

Frederick found this unacceptable. He even feared that Auld might sell him south. Once again, Frederick realized that, even as a favored slave, he had no real control over his life. He decided to try to escape.

According to legend, Anna Murray sold a feather bed to pay for Frederick Bailey's journey to freedom. She also suggested that Frederick pretend he was a sailor, and she changed his clothing to make him look the part. He also obtained papers from a free black sailor in Baltimore that showed the bearer to be a free man.

On September 3, 1838, Frederick had a friend drive him to the railroad station. He was dressed in a red shirt with a kerchief tied around his neck, and he had a sailor's flat-topped, broad-brimmed hat on his head. He boarded a train to Delaware just as it was departing. Once again, Frederick was lucky. The railroad that ran north from Baltimore was only a year old, and security was not as tight as it would be in later years.

Anna Murray, a free black woman, met Frederick Douglass when he was still a slave in Baltimore. With her help and encouragement, Douglass managed to escape to New York City, where Murray later joined him. They were married only a couple weeks after he left Maryland.

The train was crowded and going fast, but to Frederick's "anxious mind, it was moving far too slowly. Minutes were hours and hours were days." The train was almost at the Delaware border when the conductor came into the car reserved for blacks to take the passengers' tickets. Fortunately for Frederick, the conductor did not look closely at the description in the papers Frederick carried. He never noticed that the sailor who stood before him was not the man in the freedom papers.

At the Delaware border, Frederick boarded a ferry to cross the Susquehanna River. He then took a train to the city of Wilmington, Delaware, and changed there for a ferry to Philadelphia, in the free state of Pennsylvania. Three times, he saw people who knew him. Each time, he just managed to avoid trouble. From Philadelphia, he traveled to New York as quickly as possible.

"FREE EARTH UNDER MY FEET"

As he arrived in New York City, it struck Frederick that he was a free man. Walking from the ferry, he thought that the "dreams of my childhood and the purposes of my manhood were now fulfilled. A free state around me, and a free earth under my feet!" Frederick could hardly believe it. "What a moment was this to me! A whole year as pressed into a single day," he recalled. "A new world burst upon my agitated vision."

Although Frederick was thrilled by his new freedom, he still was terrified of slave catchers. (Slave catchers were people who worked for money to return escaped slaves to their owners.) The young fugitive was tired, lonely, and without money. He was afraid to trust anyone, and he spent several nights sleeping next to empty barrels on the docks. Fortunately, he met a sailor who took him to the print shop of David Ruggles. Ruggles was one of New York's most reliable members of the Underground Railroad. The Underground Railroad was a series of secret routes and safe houses for enslaved people who were escaping from slavery in the South to new lives in the North and in Canada. Ruggles sheltered Frederick and welcomed him to freedom with great celebration.

A few days after Frederick's arrival in New York, Anna Murray joined him there. Frederick and Anna were married

DAVID RUGGLES

David Ruggles (1810–1849) was Frederick Douglass' lifesaver in New York City. Ruggles was an African-American printer in New York City in the 1830s. During his 20-year career, Ruggles wrote hundreds of articles and published at least five pamphlets. His magazine, *Mirror of Liberty*, issued between 1838 and 1841, was one of the first periodicals published by a black American.

Ruggles was born in Connecticut in 1810. He was the oldest of seven children of free black parents. By 1827, he had moved to New York City. Ruggles first worked on the docks, then as a grocery shop owner, and finally as the proprietor of the nation's first black bookstore. In 1833, the *Emancipator*, an abolitionist weekly, hired him to drum up subscribers in the Middle Atlantic states.

Ruggles believed that newspapers were crucial to fighting the evil of slavery. He worried that a lack of subscriptions from blacks would doom abolitionist journalism. He urged African Americans to do their duty by supporting the *Emancipator* and other antislavery journals.

Ruggles did more than just write articles. In 1835, Ruggles and several other black activists organized the New York Committee of Vigilance. At the time, slave catchers roamed through Manhattan, looking for fugitive slaves who

in Ruggles' shop on September 15, 1838. The minister, James Pennington, also was an escaped Maryland slave. Immediately after the wedding, the newlyweds moved to New Bedford, Massachusetts. They had a letter of recommendation from Ruggles and a five-dollar bill.

had fled to the North. The Committee of Vigilance openly confronted the slave catchers. The committee demanded that New York City grant jury trials to fugitives and offered legal assistance to accused slaves. Ruggles' work with the Committee of Vigilance helped to protect the rights of local blacks.

Ruggles also was the most visible conductor on the Underground Railroad in New York City. He claimed to have helped 400 fugitive slaves during the 1830s, including Douglass in 1838. In his *Narrative*, Douglass wrote about "the humane hand of Mr. David Ruggles, whose vigilance, kindness, and perseverance I shall never forget."

The constant struggle with white racism affected Ruggles. He left New York in 1842, nearly blind and seriously ill from several diseases. A noted abolitionist author, Lydia Maria Child, arranged for Ruggles to join a radical community in Northampton, Massachusetts. There, Ruggles became a doctor of hydropathy, a water-cure treatment that was sweeping the nation. In 1845, Ruggles established the first water-cure hospital in the United States. He treated such famous abolitionists as Sojourner Truth and William Lloyd Garrison. Just as his new career soared, however, Ruggles died. The cause was a severe bowel infection; the date was December 18, 1849.

The Making of an Abolitionist

When Anna and Frederick arrived in the port of New Bedford, Massachusetts, it was one of the richest cities in the United States. The booming whaling industry made New Bedford an attractive place for free black families. In 1840, the city had a population of 12,354, of which 1,051 were black. Douglass was thrilled with his first glimpse of the docks and warehouses of New Bedford. He believed that each Northern worker seemed to have pride in his work and a sense of dignity as a human being.

Not that Massachusetts was paradise. Douglass quickly learned that color prejudice was common in the North. He could not get a job as a caulker because of discrimination against blacks. Within a week, however, he found a job loading oil onto a boat. "It was new, dirty, and hard work for me," he recalled, "but I went at it with a glad heart and a willing hand. I was now my own master. . . . It was the first work, the reward of which was to be entirely my own." For the next three years, he worked rolling oil casks, sweeping chimneys, loading ships for whaling voyages, sawing wood, shoveling coal, and picking up a job wherever he could find one. "There was no work too hard—none too dirty," he said. His wife's thriftiness and skill as a household manager also helped to ease his life as a free man.

The Douglasses began to settle into New Bedford's close-knit black community. They soon became involved with the black Methodist church. The couple's first four children were born in New Bedford: Rosetta in 1839, Lewis Henry in 1840, Frederick Jr. in 1842, and Charles Remond in 1844.

In 1841, the growing family moved to a larger house in New Bedford. Frederick seemed to find work easily in the port. There even were schools for black children. Anna worked in the garden and managed the family finances. Frederick learned to play the violin, an instrument he would love all his life. This was a world of free black families, a world without slavery. It was not unlike the world in which Anna had lived in Baltimore.

THE RISE OF ABOLITIONISM

In 1820, there were 1.5 million slaves in the United States. Organized opposition to slavery was limited to small groups of free blacks and Quakers. A group called the American Colonization Society worked to free slaves and send them back to Africa.

The situation changed in 1831. In that year, William Lloyd Garrison began to publish his newspaper, *The Liberator*. Garrison thundered that slavery was a national sin that degraded everyone and everything it touched. He demanded the immediate emancipation of all slaves. "I am in earnest," he said in *The Liberator*'s first issue. He added, "I will now equivocate—

I will not excuse—I will not retreat a single inch—AND I WILL BE HEARD!"

In about 1839, after he moved to New Bedford, Douglass subscribed to *The Liberator*. "The paper became my meat and drink," he said. "Its sympathy for my brethren in bonds—its scathing denunciations of slaveholders—its faithful exposures of slavery . . . sent a thrill of joy through my soul, such as I had

HOW FREDERICK BAILEY BECAME FREDERICK DOUGLASS

Frederick Douglass was named Frederick Augustus Washington Bailey by his mother. The Bailey name had been passed down, under various spellings, by five generations of strong black women on Maryland's Eastern Shore. Marylanders knew the young black slave as Frederick Bailey or, simply, Fred. He escaped from Baltimore under the alias Stanley. When he got to New York, he again changed his name, this time to Frederick Johnson.

On his second day in New Bedford, Frederick decided to change his name again. He was staying with a man named Nathan Johnson and decided that there were too many Johnsons in New Bedford. He gave his host "the privilege of choosing me a name, but told him he must not take from me the name of Frederick. I must hold on to that to preserve my sense of identity."

Nathan Johnson had been reading Walter Scott's best-selling poem "The Lady of the Lake." He immediately suggested the name Douglas, after one of the main characters in the romantic poem. Frederick liked the name but changed the spelling. From then on, he was known as Frederick Douglass. He never reclaimed the Bailey name, even after he purchased his freedom, when it would have been safe to do so.

Engraved by A.B. Walter, Philad.ᵃ

Douglass became an avid reader of *The Liberator*, an abolition-ist newsletter published by William Lloyd Garrison *(top)*, an ardent antislavery activist. Garrison worked with other abo-litionists, including Henry Ward Beecher, Wendell Phillips, B. Gratz Brown, Cyrus W. Field, Gerrit Smith, and Horace Greely, and hoped to end slavery for all people.

never felt before!" Douglass first heard Garrison speak on April 16, 1839, in New Bedford. He remembered the experience clearly a half century later. "I loved this paper and its editor," he said.

Garrison believed in nonviolence. He thought that abolitionists could persuade slave owners to give up their human property. He called this tactic "moral persuasion." In 1833, Garrison had joined forces with Arthur and Lewis Tappan to create the American Anti-Slavery Society (AASS). The AASS used speeches, literature, sermons, and petition drives to promote its cause. The society succeeded in transforming slavery from a relative nonissue into the most important moral crusade in American history.

Many women, both white and black, played a key role in the antislavery movement. Women's names represented more than half the signatures on AASS petitions. Women raised money for the AASS, supported abolitionist speakers, and distributed literature. The most famous members of the AASS included Lucretia Mott, Lydia Maria Child, and Abigail Kelly Foster.

Abolitionism was never a popular cause, however, because most people did not support emancipation. In 1860, out of a U.S. population of 20 million, only about 20,000 were abolitionists. Those abolitionists joined antislavery societies, where they participated in petition drives, sewing circles, and prayer groups.

The activities of abolitionists often provoked a violent response from proslavery forces. Although attacks and riots against abolitionists occurred primarily in Southern states, abuses also occurred in New York and Philadelphia. In 1835, an anti-abolitionist mob dragged Garrison through the streets of Boston with a rope around his neck, as the mob yelled, "Lynch him."

A MAN! A MAN!

The Douglass family was doing well in New Bedford, but Frederick yearned for something more. He wanted to put his slave past behind him. He also wanted to tell his story. His first recorded speech was at a church meeting in March 1839. *The Liberator* reported that a "Mr. Douglass" had spoken and had told the audience why slaves should be set free to live in the United States, not sent back to Africa. Douglass attended other antislavery meetings and began to describe his experiences as a slave.

In August 1841, the Massachusetts Anti-Slavery Society held a summer meeting on the island of Nantucket. Several of the stars of the AASS attended, including William Lloyd Garrison, Wendell Phillips, and Parker Pillsbury. Douglass also attended. On August 16, 1841, he "felt strongly moved to speak."

Douglass told the audience the story of his life. It was the story of a slave who had learned to read, had studied *The Columbian Orator*, had fled to the North, and now was speaking to important people in Massachusetts. His speech was well received, but most reports of the night focus on Garrison's response after Douglass finished speaking. Deeply moved by Douglass' tale, Garrison asked the audience, "Have we been listening to a thing, a chattel personal, or a man?" The audience shouted, "A man! A man!" Garrison went on, "Shall such a man be held a slave in a Christian land?" "No! No!" shouted the audience. Rising to full voice, Garrison asked, "Shall such a man ever be sent back to bondage from the free soil of old Massachusetts?" With a tremendous roar, the whole meeting rose to its feet and chanted, "No! No! No!"

Suddenly, Douglass was a star. He was not the first former slave to speak for the antislavery movement. He soon became the most famous African-American abolitionist, however.

ANTISLAVERY LECTURER

The Massachusetts Anti-Slavery Society quickly hired Douglass as a speaker. Douglass traveled widely, spending months away from his wife and young children. During the next two years, Douglass spoke at antislavery meetings in more than 100 towns, villages, and cities in New England, New York, Ohio, Indiana, and Pennsylvania. In general, Douglass' lectures were a great success. He often drew large crowds. People wanted to see and hear the former slave. Douglass seemed to outshine even Garrison.

Antislavery speakers sometimes faced hostile crowds. Angry mobs pelted AASS speakers with rotten vegetables and rocks. In 1843, in Pendleton, Indiana, a proslavery mob physically assaulted Douglass and two white abolitionists.

Abolitionists were incredibly determined and energetic, however. They were not easily discouraged. Physical attacks and bombardment with rotten eggs just further convinced them that they were right. Americans who thought or hoped that the issue of slavery would go away began to realize that nothing would silence the antislavery speakers. They would keep talking until slavery ended.

Douglass preached against slavery the Garrisonian way. This meant that he insisted on nonviolence. In 1843, Douglass attended the National Convention of Colored Citizens. At this meeting, Douglass argued against black abolitionist Henry Highland Garnet's call for slaves to use violence against their masters. According to a summary of the meeting, Douglass stated that he feared Garnet's advice "would lead to an insurrection. . . . He [Douglass] was for trying the moral means a little longer."

Following Garrison's lead, Douglass declared that the United States Constitution was a proslavery document. He refused to cooperate with any political party, even an antislavery one such as the Liberty Party (formed in 1840). For Garrison and for Douglass, politics was corrupting, evil, and to be avoided.

Douglass also criticized the twin movements of colonization and emigrationism. Colonization was a movement promoted by some whites who supported emancipation as long as the freed slaves left the United States and went to Africa or to the Caribbean. Emigrationism, on the other hand, was a movement led by blacks. The emigrationists had concluded that,

Douglass met Henry Highland Garnet *(above)* during his early years in the abolitionist movement. Douglass, who was seen as a protégé of William Lloyd Garrison, disagreed and argued against Garnet's encouragement for slaves to attain freedom through violence or emigration back to Africa.

because white racism would never end in the United States, blacks would be better off moving to some other country. Douglass hated both of these movements, which he considered almost identical. When the black abolitionists Henry Highland Garnet and Martin Delany supported a "back to Africa" movement, Douglass attacked them with the same ferocity that he used against the white-led American Colonization Society.

AN ORATOR IN AN AGE OF ORATORY

The 1800s were an age of oratory, the art of formal speaking to an audience. Oratory was a form of entertainment. Nineteenth-century audiences enjoyed listening to speeches for hours on end.

Oratory also represented the power to persuade. Speakers in the 1800s did not rely on gimmicks or special effects. They

HENRY HIGHLAND GARNET

Henry Highland Garnet (1815–1882), like Frederick Douglass, was an escaped slave from the Eastern Shore of Maryland. In New York City, Garnet attended the African Free School. He then studied at the Noyes Academy in New Hampshire. The white farmers of the region resented the presence of blacks. They formed violent mobs and forced Garnet to flee. He was then a student at the abolitionist Oneida Institute in Whitestown, New York. In 1839, Garnet moved to Troy, New York, and became a pastor at a black Presbyterian Church. He also lectured for the AASS and campaigned for the Liberty Party.

Garnet was one of the most outspoken abolitionists, white or black. In 1843, he gave a famous speech entitled "Call to Rebellion" to the National Convention of Free Colored Persons in Buffalo. In this speech, Garnet urged the black slaves of the South to demand freedom, even if this meant using violence. He closed his speech by saying, "Brethren, arise, arise. Strike for your lives and liberties.

used words and sentences to carry content and meaning to their audiences. Orators assumed, correctly, that most nineteenth-century listeners knew current events. When Douglass spoke, he wanted to impress and entertain. Most of all, though, he wanted to persuade people that slavery was evil and needed to be abolished.

Douglass was the star of the antislavery lecturers. He attracted as many listeners as William Lloyd Garrison. Audiences considered Douglass handsome and distinguished-

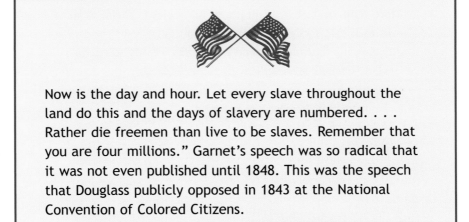

Now is the day and hour. Let every slave throughout the land do this and the days of slavery are numbered. . . . Rather die freemen than live to be slaves. Remember that you are four millions." Garnet's speech was so radical that it was not even published until 1848. This was the speech that Douglass publicly opposed in 1843 at the National Convention of Colored Citizens.

Garnet believed that black abolitionists had to control the antislavery struggle themselves instead of deferring to whites. Garnet wrote of white abolitionists, "They are our allies—ours is the battle." In the 1850s, Garnet grew discouraged and began to support voluntary black emigration. "I would rather see a man free in Liberia than a slave in the United States," he said. In 1858, Garnet started the African Civilization Society and began preaching in New York City. His support for emigration put him in direct opposition to Douglass. During the Civil War, he recruited black troops for the Union Army. In later years, he became active in the Republican Party. He was appointed U.S. minister to Liberia in 1881.

looking. He had a powerful build; deep-set, flashing eyes; and a mass of hair crowning his head. When he spoke in his rich, baritone voice, he roared and waved his arms. He used sarcasm, ridicule, and mimicry to devastating effect. He also could be quite funny when he felt like it. Douglass' passion excited his listeners. He amazed them with his verbal skill. He also shocked them with his gruesome stories of slavery.

Douglass' speeches averaged two hours in length. Yet for more than 50 years, large crowds gathered to hear Douglass speak. One listener reported that Douglass was:

> More than six feet in height, and his majestic form, as he rose to speak, straight as an arrow, muscular, yet lithe and graceful, his flashing eye, and more than all, his voice, that rivaled [Daniel] Webster's in its richness, and in the depth and sonorousness of its cadences, made up such an ideal of an orator as the listeners never forgot.

Abolitionist and social activist Elizabeth Cady Stanton described a Douglass lecture in 1842:

> Around him sat the great antislavery orators of the day, watching the effect of his eloquence on that immense audience that laughed and wept by turns, completely carried away by the wondrous gifts of his pathos and humor. . . . [He] stood there like an African prince, majestic in his wrath.

Douglass paid no attention to abolitionist and reformer Parker Pillsbury's advice that it was "better [to] have a little of the plantation" in his speech. Even Garrison warned him that he should not sound too "learned," or people would not "believe you were ever a slave." Instead, Douglass astonished audiences with his learning and diction. An amazed listener expressed admiration for "the magnetism and melody of [Douglass'] wonderfully elastic voice. . . . No orator we have ever heard can use with such grace, eloquence, and effect as he."

In fact, Douglass was too good. One abolitionist heard him speak in Philadelphia in 1844. He wrote to Garrison:

> Many persons in the audience seemed unable to credit the statements which he [Douglass] gave of himself, and could not believe that he was actually a slave. How a man, only six years out of bondage, and who had never gone to school a day in his life, could speak with such eloquence—such precision of language and power of thought—they were utterly at a loss to devise.

The *Narrative*

In 1842, Douglass moved his family to Lynn, Massachusetts. Lynn was a small town just north of Boston. Living in Lynn put Douglass very close to the Boston abolitionists. It also provided him with a safe place to write his autobiography *Narrative of the Life of Frederick Douglass, An American Slave, Written by Himself.*

By 1844, many people who heard Douglass speak did not believe that he was who he said he was. They insisted that his intelligence, language, and poise proved that he was not a self-educated former slave. Douglass admitted that proslavery people "might have persisted in representing me as an imposter, a free negro, who had never been south of the Mason and Dixon's line; whom the abolitionists had educated, and sent forth as a fugitive slave, to attract attention to their faltering cause." There actually had been a few cases of that sort.

NARRATIVE

OF THE

LIFE

OF

FREDERICK DOUGLASS,

AN

AMERICAN SLAVE.

WRITTEN BY HIMSELF.

BOSTON:
PUBLISHED AT THE ANTI-SLAVERY OFFICE,
No. 25 Cornhill
1845.

Frederick Douglass

To prove he really was a former slave, Frederick Douglass wrote his autobiography, *Narrative of the Life of Frederick Douglass, An American Slave, Written by Himself*. As a runaway slave, Douglass' decision to print his real name and the name of his master put his family and himself at risk.

Douglass felt that he had to reveal the details of his life as a slave. Abolitionists, especially Wendell Phillips, encouraged him to write his life story. This would mean giving his slave name and disclosing the identities of his masters. Such information could put his freedom at risk and his family in trouble. It was a decision that took a great deal of courage.

Through the winter of 1844–1845, Douglass lectured mostly in eastern Massachusetts. This left him time to finish writing his book, which he completed in April 1845. William Lloyd Garrison, who edited the book, did not make many changes. He wrote that Douglass had "chosen to write his own *Narrative*, in his own style, and according to the best of his ability, rather than to employ someone else. It is, therefore, entirely his own production." Many people had heard Douglass lecture. They knew that the language of the *Narrative* was the same as Douglass' language when he told his story as a speaker.

SLAVE NARRATIVES

Slave narratives told the personal experiences of African Americans who had escaped from slavery. They first appeared in England in the 1700s. Soon, they became a basic part of the antislavery movement. In the 1800s, autobiographies of former slaves were the most common form of African-American writing.

About 65 American slave narratives were published before 1865. Some were bestsellers. William Wells Brown's *Narrative* went through four editions in its first year. Solomon Northup's *Twelve Years a Slave* sold 27,000 copies in two years. Slave narratives were translated into French, German, Dutch, and Russian. Although these books were widely read, it is unclear how much they affected American attitudes toward slavery.

Slave narratives appealed to white readers' desire for romantic and sensational stories. The horror and violence of a slave's life fascinated Northerners. These stories also provided interesting and sometimes detailed descriptions of life in the South. This was important in an age before television.

Slave narratives gave Northerners a glimpse into the lives of enslaved black men, women, and children. The narratives showed the horrors of family separation, the cruelty

The Massachusetts Anti-Slavery Society published the first edition of the 125-page *Narrative* in Boston in 1845. The book sold for 50 cents. By fall, the society had sold 4,500 copies. Soon, there were three European editions. Within five years, the book went through 20 editions and sold 30,000 copies. Douglass sold it before and after his speeches to help to pay his expenses.

of individual slave owners, and the sexual abuse of black women. They told of free blacks being kidnapped and sold into slavery. They described the brutality of whipping and the severe living conditions of slave life. They also told exciting tales of escape, heroism, betrayal, and tragedy. The narratives portrayed black people as fascinating and sympathetic characters.

Some famous North American slave narratives include:

Slavery in the United States: A Narrative of the Life and Adventures of Charles Ball, A Black Man (1836)
Narrative of William Wells Brown, an American Slave (1849)
Narrative of the Life and Adventures of Henry Bibb, an American Slave (1849)
Twelve Years a Slave: Narrative of Solomon Northup (1853)
Incidents in the Life of a Slave Girl [Harriet Jacobs] (1861)

It may sound silly, but slave narratives showed whites that African Americans were people. These narratives proved to whites that blacks could master language and write their own history. Abolitionists used slave narratives as weapons. They hoped the tales would arouse the sympathy of readers and convince them to fight against slavery.

Douglass' autobiography was far more widely read then Henry David Thoreau's *Walden* or Walt Whitman's *Leaves of Grass*. The publication of the *Narrative* made the 27-year-old Douglass a national celebrity. He became one of the first African Americans to gain the interest of a nationwide white audience.

ESTABLISHING HIS CREDIBILITY

One of the reasons Douglass wrote his autobiography was to prove that he actually had been a slave. To do this, he had to establish his credibility. He wanted people to believe his story.

Narrative of the Life of Frederick Douglass contained a photograph of Douglass on its first page [see page 57]. A copy of Douglass' signature was printed below the photograph. Before a reader even began the book, he or she saw a picture of the author and proof that he was literate.

There was a ten-page preface by Garrison and a four-page letter from Wendell Phillips. These two famous white abolitionists guaranteed that Douglass was not lying. They discussed his many sufferings and his great accomplishments. They showed tremendous enthusiasm for Douglass and for his story. The *Narrative,* Phillips argued, gave "a fair specimen of the whole truth. No one-sided portrait, —no wholesale complaints, —but strict justice done."

Most importantly, Douglass used real names when he referred to people and places in Maryland. He described whippings and murders. His courage was astounding. As an escaped slave, he was still Thomas Auld's property. When the book reached the public, slave catchers could kidnap him and return him to the South at any moment.

The *Narrative* created a sensation in Maryland. It was widely read despite strict laws against spreading abolitionist propaganda. Some local people claimed that Douglass lied about his experiences to make a stronger case against slavery. The Aulds were enraged at what they considered slander. No one denied, however, that the author was, in fact, Freddy Bailey, once a slave from the sleepy Eastern Shore.

STYLE AND THEME OF THE NARRATIVE

Douglass knew the style of slave narratives when he started to write his own. Between 1838 and 1844, Douglass had read many antislavery publications. These contained speeches, interviews, and autobiographies of dozens of fugitive slaves. Douglass used this type of material to shape his own story.

Douglass turned his story into a spiritual journey. The first chapter established the author's existence although he had no birth date or family history. The innocent boy entered through "the blood-stained gate, the entrance to the hell of slavery." That "hell" included descriptions of cruel masters, evil overseers, brutal whippings, and other atrocities of slave life. Slowly, the author grew in moral strength because of his suffering. He decided to resist, fought his master, failed at one escape attempt, and then succeeded at another.

Douglass did not end his story with his escape, however. The last chapter of the *Narrative* describes his arrival into the heavenly paradise of Northern middle-class life: freedom, a job, and a wife. Douglass did not believe that the goal of a fugitive slave was simply to escape. He ended his story with his taking up a new identity as a free American man. The *Narrative* concludes with his antislavery speech at Nantucket. Douglass knew that to add this last detail was to recast Garrison and Phillips as minor characters in Douglass' own story.

Douglass wrote his *Narrative* in a simple and direct style. The book has almost no quoted passages. It rarely refers to other famous books. The details are usually concrete. This direct style appealed to readers in the 1800s and continues to appeal to readers today. As Douglass grew older, however, he gradually abandoned this direct style.

The central theme of the *Narrative* is one of human struggle. Douglass describes in detail how he suffered under slavery. The slave system almost reduces him to a beast of labor. Gradually, he manages to restore his manhood by learning to read and by standing up to Edward Covey. He struggles to resist temptations such as drinking alcohol. As he grows,

Douglass stays focused on his goals of morality, wisdom, and freedom. The *Narrative* relates a tale of growing self-confidence and growing self-reliance. From a small beginning, Douglass seems almost to create himself by acts of sheer willpower.

Douglass does not write much about the day-to-day details of slave life in the *Narrative*. Compared with other slave narratives, Douglass' *Narrative* has little to say about slave quarters, diet, work life, holidays, and family relations. Douglass did not want to explain the slave experience. His primary purpose was to provide evidence against the evil of slavery. He wanted his book to awaken the reader's sympathy. If Douglass was successful in this, the reader would join him in the fight for human freedom.

WRITTEN BY HIMSELF

Douglass also had a personal goal in writing the *Narrative*. He wanted to take control of his own story. For several years, the Boston abolitionists had been telling him what to say and how to understand it. He was not quite ready to separate from the Garrisonians. In the *Narrative*, however, he makes it clear that he intends to tell his own story in his own way.

The subtitle of the *Narrative* is "Written by Himself." This looks, at first, like a simple addition to the title. These three words actually carry great weight, however. Slaves were not supposed to be able to read and write. "Written by Himself" is the proud claim of a self-made man. A piece of property cannot write a narrative. The words serve as an attack on slave owners who tried to prevent enslaved people from reading and writing. The words also are a statement of warning to the Boston abolitionists. Douglass was intent on keeping control of his own life story.

In his story, Douglass refuses to tell the details of his escape. He writes that he does not want to endanger anyone who helped him. His refusal to speak about this also is a way to tell his own story. Only Douglass could tell (or refuse to tell) about his escape. Garrison and Phillips did not know the story, so they could not tell it. In fact, Douglass did not relate the details until 1881, long after it became safe to do so.

THE TRIP TO GREAT BRITAIN

In 1845, about three months after the publication of the *Narrative*, Douglass sailed for Great Britain. He said that "he wanted to be out of the way during the excitement" after the publication of his book. He also feared capture by slave hunters.

In addition, an international audience existed that wanted to hear Douglass speak. British antislavery societies had not closed down after the British abolished slavery in 1833. The movement remained strong in Great Britain. Close ties existed among abolitionists on both sides of the Atlantic.

The trip was a personal triumph for Douglass. He made impressive antislavery speeches in England, Ireland, and Scotland. He called on Christians to join the abolitionist movement and to stop associating with slave owners. He sold hundreds of copies of the *Narrative* at his lectures. Douglass became a celebrity in Great Britain. He even thought briefly about moving to Scotland or England.

Meanwhile, Hugh Auld was angered by Douglass' depiction of his family in the *Narrative*. In 1845, he bought Douglass from Thomas Auld. Abolitionists spread the rumor that Hugh meant to recapture and punish his former slave if Douglass returned to the United States.

In 1846, two British abolitionists decided to buy Douglass from Auld. They offered 150 pounds (about $1,000) that they had raised from British antislavery supporters. Auld took the money and signed the manumission (freedom) papers. Douglass was a free man. Some abolitionists criticized Douglass for allowing the abolitionists to pay a ransom for his freedom. Douglass said that he preferred to be a free antislavery speaker than a possible martyr to the cause of freedom.

Concerned over his safety and freedom, Frederick Douglass (depicted above) completed a two-year speaking tour of Great Britain after the publication of his autobiography. While overseas, antislavery groups raised enough money to purchase Douglass' freedom, alleviating his fears of capture by slave hunters.

MY OLD MASTER

In his lectures and in his books, Douglass made the names of Hugh and Thomas Auld into symbols of evil on two continents. "Bad as slaveholders are," Douglass wrote in the *Narrative*, "I have seldom met with one so destitute of every element of character capable of inspiring respect, as was my present master, Capt. Thomas Auld." Douglass concluded, "When I lived with him, I thought him incapable of a noble action. The leading trait in his character was an intense selfishness."

In 1848, Douglass continued his attack by writing a public letter to Thomas Auld. Douglass published the letter in his own newspaper, the *North Star,* to celebrate the tenth anniversary of his flight to freedom. In his letter, Douglass warned Auld not to expect fair treatment from him. He wrote, "I intend to make use of you as a weapon with which to assail the system of slavery."

Douglass' attacks on the Aulds only disguise the complex relationship he had with his white masters. Douglass had to break with Thomas Auld to break with slavery. Douglass presented Auld as a cruel and evil slave owner because Douglass was willing to use any weapon to destroy slavery. In his *Narrative* and "Letter to My Old Master," Douglass marshaled a collection of horrors that young Frederick Bailey suffered under slavery. Some of the accusations against Auld were true, some were half true, and some were outright lies.

Douglass suffered greatly under slavery. He never knew his mother or his father. His brothers and sisters were strangers to him. White owners bought and sold him, and they put a dollar value on him. He was whipped and beaten. White masters forced him to work and then stole his pay. He was deprived of an education as a child. As a young man, white people beat him simply because of his skin color. In addition, there was the mental strain of his fate. He had to live with the knowledge that he would forever be a slave, as would his children and his grandchildren. He had no hope and no future other than endless work to make other people rich.

Yet, without minimizing his horrible situation, it is important to remember that, from early childhood, several white masters recognized Frederick Bailey as an extremely gifted boy.

DOUGLASS' REUNIONS WITH THE AULDS

After the Civil War, Frederick Douglass had several emotional reunions with African-American family members. Unfortunately, Douglass noted that his brothers and sisters were like strangers to him. In his final autobiography, however, Douglass devoted several pages to a discussion of his reunions with the "white branch" of his family. These people obviously were equally important to him.

In 1877, Douglass returned home to Talbot County for the first time in 41 years. He wanted to patch up his relationship with Thomas Auld, who finally had agreed to meet with him. Auld, 82 years old and dying, was in St. Michaels.

When the two old adversaries finally met, the first thing Douglass asked Auld was about his reaction to Frederick's escape. "Frederick," Auld replied, "I always knew you were too smart to be a slave, and had I been in your place, I should have done as you did." Douglass replied, "Capt. Auld, I am glad to hear you say this. I did not run away from you, but from slavery."

Douglass then apologized to Auld for claiming that Auld had cruelly mistreated Douglass' grandmother. In fact, in 1840, when Auld learned that Harriet Bailey was ill, he sent

At the Wye House, he was the chosen companion of Colonel Lloyd's son. For seven important years during his youth, he lived with a mistress who treated him almost like a foster son. He was fortunate enough to live in the exciting environment of Baltimore. Three times, the Aulds had to make major decisions

for her and cared for her in his home until her death. Then Auld and Douglass briefly discussed the date of Frederick's birth. Their entire interview took only 20 minutes.

Younger African Americans criticized Douglass for meeting with Auld. Many blacks thought that Douglass had gone soft on white people. Douglass, as usual, did what he pleased. He told his critics that the scars on his back and his years in the abolitionist movement spoke for him. It was clear, however, that, except as a symbol of slave owners, Douglass had never hated Auld at all.

Douglass also kept in touch with Amanda Auld Sears, the only child of Thomas and Lucretia Auld. He met her in 1859 in Philadelphia, and Douglass and Sears maintained a warm friendship until her death in 1878. He also regularly wrote to her children.

In 1881, Douglass revisited the Lloyd Plantation. To Douglass' own amazement, he enjoyed sipping wine on the patio with Lloyd's grandchildren. He had come full circle from his childhood a half-century before. Then, he had been Freddy Bailey, the ragged slave boy sneaking looks at distinguished visitors to Wye House. Now, he sat on the veranda, the greatest orator in the United States. As Douglass noted in his final autobiography, "Time makes all things even."

that affected Frederick Bailey's future. Each time, they decided to send him back to Baltimore to live with the gentle Sophia Auld.

Douglass sometimes called himself "a favored slave." He wrote about his childhood, "I was seldom whipped by my old master, and suffered little from anything else than hunger and cold." He lived at the Lloyd plantation only 18 months out of his 20 years of slavery in Maryland. Although the Lloyds were brutal slave owners, Frederick's main problem—hunger—was caused by the black cook. In Baltimore, for seven years, Douglass wrote, "I got few whippings, and few slaves could boast of a kinder master or mistress than myself." Only during his seven months under Edward Covey did Frederick experience the full horrors of slavery as millions of blacks experienced it.

This does not minimize what Douglass suffered under slavery. It was the institution of slavery, not individual slave owners, that Douglass hated. In his *Narrative*, Douglass wanted to show that slavery corrupted everything and everyone associated with it, including the slave owner. For example, in the *Narrative*, Sophia initially is described as a kind woman. When she becomes a slave owner, "the fatal poison of irresponsible power" turns her into a demon. Douglass wrote, "Slavery proved as injurious to her as it did to me."

In 1858, Douglass wrote to Hugh Auld. "I ran away not from you, but from slavery," Douglass wrote. "Indeed, I feel nothing but kindness for you all." Twenty years after his escape, he wrote, "I love you, but hate slavery." Douglass also kept a tremendous affection for Sophia. During the Civil War, he tried to visit her in Baltimore. He wrote to Hugh, "Gladly would I see you and Mrs. Auld—or Miss Sophia, as I used to call her." Douglass' letter went unanswered. In fact, it was the Aulds who did not want to meet with Douglass. The former masters still were offended by the things their former slave had said and written about them.

The Burned-over
District

Whaen Douglass returned to the United States from Great
Britain, he decided to strike out on his own. He longed
to bring his ideas on the slavery question before the public. "I
seem to have undergone a transformation," he told William
Lloyd Garrison. "I live a new life." Douglass moved his family
from Massachusetts to the city of Rochester in upstate New
York. Douglass wanted to edit his own newspaper. Friends in
Great Britain had raised several thousand dollars to help him.

Garrison's group of Boston abolitionists was not happy with
this plan. They knew that Douglass was a great speaker. They
wanted him to continue lecturing for the AASS. They worried
that a new abolitionist newspaper would hurt the always-
struggling *Liberator*.

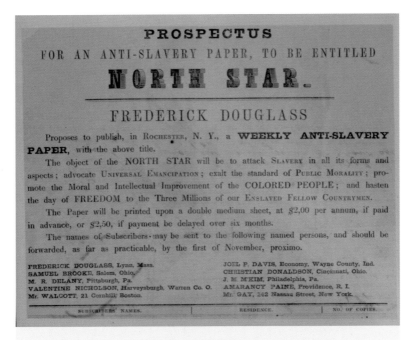

The *North Star*, Frederick Douglass' newspaper, was meant to encourage abolitionism and education among free blacks. Douglass named his paper after the actual North Star, which served as an astronomical guide to runaway slaves on the Underground Railroad. Above, the prospectus, or mission statement, of the North Star.

The Boston abolitionists also were jealous and, perhaps, racist. They resented Douglass' confidence and thought that he was ungrateful. Douglass' newspaper plans especially offended Garrison. He wrote that Douglass' "conduct grieves me to the heart. His conduct . . . has been impulsive [and] inconsiderate."

In October 1847, Douglass wrote to a friend, "I have finally decided on publishing the *North Star* [his newspaper] in Rochester and to make that city my future home." Douglass wanted his newspaper "to elevate and improve the condition" of free blacks in the United States. Douglass also wanted African Americans to run their own businesses and to be "our own representatives and advocates." He hired the black abolitionist Martin Delany as coeditor and an all-black staff. The first edition of the *North Star* appeared on December 3, 1847, in the middle of the Mexican-American War.

At its peak, the *North Star* had about 3,000 subscribers, but the subscriptions barely covered the printing costs. Douglass was frustrated because white subscribers outnumbered black by about a five-to-one margin. He felt as if he was not reaching most African Americans in the North. Soon, Douglass had to lecture on the road again to raise money.

PERFECTIONISM IN UPSTATE NEW YORK

Douglass lived in Rochester for 25 years. The city was a center of reform in the so-called "burned-over district." This was the nickname given to this region of central and western New York State during the period from 1800 to 1860 when the area was affected by wave after wave of religious excitement.

Rochester had boomed after the completion of the Erie Canal in 1825. By 1847, it was a prosperous manufacturing center with a population of 50,000. The city also was one of the last stops on the Underground Railroad. Rochester's white and black citizens helped many runaway slaves flee the United States to find freedom in Canada.

In the early 1800s, a Christian movement known as the Second Great Awakening spread across the United States. Preachers such as Charles Grandison Finney and Lyman Beecher spoke of a very personal relationship with a friendly God. They taught that human beings have free choice in moral decisions. In many areas, camp meeting–style preaching drew thousands of people.

Great numbers of Americans tried to put their religious principles into action. They wanted to improve society. They were inspired by Jesus' words at the conclusion of the Sermon on the Mount: "You must, therefore, be perfect as your heavenly

(continues on page 74)

THE MANY LIVES OF MARTIN DELANY (1812–1885)

The paths of Frederick Douglass and Martin Delany crossed many times during their lives, sometimes as friends and sometimes as foes. Delany's influence was widespread. At one time or another, he worked as an abolitionist, a doctor, an editor, a novelist, a judge, and a soldier. In any position he held, Delany always was proud to have dark skin.

Delany was born free in Virginia in 1812. In 1831, he moved to Pittsburgh, Pennsylvania, attended Jefferson College, and learned Latin and Greek. In 1843, Delany began publishing *The Mystery*, a black-supported news-paper. He also was active in the antislavery movement.

Douglass and Delany worked together as coeditors of the *North Star*. For 18 months, Delany traveled through the Midwest, lecturing, reporting, and gathering subscrip-tions. The two men were still friendly in 1850, when Delany was accepted to study medicine at Harvard University. The month after his arrival, however, a group of white Harvard students petitioned their professors. The students claimed that "the admission of blacks to the medical lectures [is] highly detrimental to the interests, and welfare of the Institution of which we are members." Within three weeks, Harvard dismissed Delany and his fellow black students. This incident convinced Delany that white racism always would oppress blacks in the United States. His opinions became more radical.

In 1852, Delany wrote *The Condition, Elevation, Emigration, and Destiny of the Colored People of the*

United States. In it, he argued that blacks had no future in the country. He suggested that they should leave and found a new nation in Africa. In 1854, Delany led the first National Emigration Convention in Cleveland, Ohio. Five years later, he traveled to western Africa for nine months, to investigate possible sites for a new black nation of African-American settlers. Douglass hated the idea of emigrationism and often attacked Delany's ideas during the 1850s.

Delany abandoned his emigrationist ideas when the Civil War began. He joined Douglass in recruiting black soldiers for the U.S. Army. In 1865, Delany met with President Abraham Lincoln, who described Delany as "this most extraordinary and intelligent man." A few weeks later, Delany was commissioned as a major, thereby becoming the first black field officer in the U.S. Army.

As if all this were not enough, during the years 1859–1862, Delany also published a serialized novel entitled *Blake*. The story dealt with a black revolutionary's secret travels through slave communities in the South. *Blake* was one of the first novels by a black man to be published in America.

After the Civil War, Delany jumped into the complicated politics of South Carolina. He shocked whites with his call for land for former slaves. He shocked blacks by supporting the Democratic Party. By the late 1870s, Delany again grew discouraged with racism in the South. Once again, he backed the idea of emigration to Africa. In 1885, after a life filled with twists and turns, Delany died of tuberculosis.

(continued from page 71)
Father is perfect" (Matthew 5:48). Many Christian Americans of the early 1800s took this statement literally. They were known as perfectionists.

These new beliefs attracted thousands of people in New England, New York, and Ohio. They helped to drive reform movements such as the antislavery, women's rights, and temperance (opposition to drinking alcohol) movements. Abolitionists and Christian perfectionist ministers shared many of the same techniques of persuasion. Both groups relied on traveling speakers, camp meetings, petitions, and pamphlets to get out the word.

Many notable African Americans lived in the burned-over district. Ministers Samuel May and Jermain Longuen came from Syracuse. Other black leaders such as Henry Highland Garnet, William Wells Brown, and Harriet Tubman made the burned-over district their home. Noted white abolitionist leaders such as Gerrit Smith, who lived in Peterboro, and William Seward, of Auburn, joined them there. When Douglass moved to Rochester, he moved to the most reform-minded area of the United States.

A TROUBLED MARRIAGE

Anna, Douglass' wife, remained in Lynn during his tour of Great Britain. She supported herself by working at home, sewing shoes on a piecework basis. She also belonged to the Lynn Ladies' Anti-Slavery Society. Anna was a strong and determined partner. She loyally supported Douglass and skillfully managed their household. She raised three sons and two daughters almost entirely without her husband's help.

After traveling for 10 years in the North, Douglass had changed, however. He was no longer a day laborer but an orator, a writer, and an editor. Anna, meanwhile, acted more like a servant than the wife of a famous man. She often retreated into the kitchen after greeting visitors. Douglass met people from every class of society. Anna was naturally quiet and never at ease in white company. She almost never appeared at her husband's speeches. Douglass especially disliked the fact that Anna never learned to read or write. He loved to read. He believed that literacy opened the road to freedom and that illiteracy equaled ignorance.

Their 44-year marriage does not seem to have been a happy one. The last of their five children, a girl they named Annie, was born in March 1849. In Douglass' autobiographies, he barely mentions his wife. She receives less than five sentences in each of his two later autobiographies, both of which are more than 400 pages long. In 1846, Douglass revealingly wrote to a relative, "It would spread a dark cloud over my soul to see you marry some ignorant and unlearned person. You might as well tie yourself to a log of wood as to do so. You are altogether too refined and intelligent a person for any such marriage." Unconsciously, Douglass probably felt himself "tied to a log."

Douglass first met Julia Griffiths during his European tour. She was a young, single, white Englishwoman who was both intelligent and energetic. The two developed an intense and lasting friendship. In 1849, Griffiths came to the United States to work with Douglass in Rochester. She edited the *North Star* and helped it to survive while Douglass traveled on his lecture tours. For seven years, Griffiths served as Douglass' business manager, fund-raiser, and editorial assistant.

The relationship between Douglass and Griffiths became a scandal. It was not because he was married and she was not, but because he was black and she was white. Most whites in America hated the idea of interracial relationships. They thought they were unnatural or evil. Many abolitionists worried that this relationship would lead to accusations of miscegenation (interracial marriage or sex), which would hurt the antislavery cause.

Douglass tried not to let anyone's disapproval intimidate him. By 1855, however, the criticism had become so intense that Griffiths felt she had to leave Rochester. She returned to England, where she continued her many antislavery activities. Until her death, almost a half-century later, she never stopped writing to her "beloved friend."

FIGHTING PREJUDICE IN THE NORTH

When Douglass first came to the North, he compared the "free states" to heaven. The *Narrative* ends with his arrival in this "Promised Land." The book is very quiet about Northern racism. Douglass experienced many humiliating episodes in the North because of his skin color, however.

Douglass could not find a caulker's job in New Bedford because he was black. He could not ride Boston's omnibuses. At theaters, lecture halls, and most churches, he had to sit in the back or in the balcony with other African Americans. His children could not attend public schools with white children. In many states, he would not have been able to vote. In New York State, where all white men could vote, blacks had to meet a high property qualification. It was not even socially acceptable for white and black people to walk down the street together.

As a result of these daily indignities, Douglass began to criticize discrimination in the North. He objected to American racism, especially after his return from England, where color prejudice was not so extreme. Douglass linked the struggle for emancipation in the South with the struggle for equality in the North. Douglass closed his first recorded speech with these words: "Prejudice against color is stronger north than south; it hangs around my neck like a heavy weight . . . and I have met it at every step the three years I have been out of southern slavery."

In August 1848, Douglass' oldest daughter enrolled in Seward Seminary in Rochester. Douglass was in Cleveland when she began school. When he returned, he found out that the school had forbidden Rosetta to sit with the other girls. Douglass was enraged. He protested to the school's principal "against the cruelty and injustice of treating [my] child as a criminal on account of her color." Nonetheless, he could not convince the board of trustees to change the policy. His daughter had to transfer to another school. Douglass began a fight to desegregate Rochester's public schools, a struggle that finally succeeded in 1857.

DOUGLASS AND CHRISTIANITY

As a youth, Frederick Bailey had been powerfully drawn to religion. Sophia had read to him from the Bible when he was a child. As a young man, he had found spiritual inspiration in the words of a series of ministers.

Douglass' faith gradually drifted away, however. He grew disillusioned and then disgusted with American Christianity. He especially condemned the churches for their hypocrisy. He saved his bitterest sarcasm for churches that defended slavery and racial prejudice even as they preached universal goodwill. "The religion of the South is a mere covering for the most horrid crimes," Douglass thundered. It was "a justifier of the most appalling barbarity,— a sanctifier of the most hateful frauds,— and a dark shelter, under which the darkest, foulest, grossest, and most infernal deeds of slaveholders find the strongest protection. . . . Of all slaveholders with whom I have ever met, religious slaveholders are the worst."

Douglass ended the *Narrative* with a vicious attack on Christianity as white people practiced it in the United States. He did, however, draw a distinction between American Christianity and the Christianity of Christ. "I love the pure, peaceable, and impartial Christianity of Christ," he said. "I

In addition to condemning American Christianity in his autobiography, Douglass criticized the black church and black ministers for not doing enough to end slavery. Douglass desired an integrated church or organization like the Anti-Slavery Society where blacks would be exposed to different kinds of religious education instead of what he saw as going along with the status quo.

therefore hate the corrupt, slaveholding, women-whipping, cradle-plundering, partial, and hypocritical Christianity of this land."

These attacks angered most Americans. Still, many abolitionists joined Douglass in proclaiming the guilt of organized religion. They knew that churches often obstructed antislavery meetings and tried to silence the lectures of abolitionist speakers.

Douglass did not shy away from criticizing black churches and black ministers. He felt that they were too cautious on racial issues. When slavery finally was abolished, Douglass declared that there was no reason to thank God, because abolition resulted from human effort. He attacked the black churches that "led everything against the abolition of slavery, always holding us back by telling us that God would abolish slavery in his own good time." Black ministers were scandalized.

Douglass believed in the power of reason. He did not believe in miracles. "Schooled as I have been among the abolitionists of New England," he wrote, "I recognize that the universe is governed by laws which are unchangeable and eternal." He concluded his last autobiography by noting that "All the prayers of Christendom cannot stop the force of a single bullet."

Douglass never abandoned the church, however. Although he hated Christian hypocrisy, he was unwilling to part with the faith that had guided him since his childhood. Until his death, Douglass frequently used religious terms and biblical images in his speeches.

THE FREE-SOIL PARTY

William Lloyd Garrison refused to work with any political party. He believed that the corruption of politics would soil the purity of the antislavery message. The result, he believed, would be an evil compromise. Garrison and his followers also denounced the American Constitution as "a pact with the devil" because it recognized and protected slavery. The Garrisonian motto was "No Union with Slaveholders."

Douglass was never a wholehearted Garrisonian. He did not see how letting the Southern states secede—withdraw from the United States—could possibly help the slaves. By the late 1840s, Douglass considered any effort to eliminate slavery to be worthwhile. At the Women's Rights Covention in Seneca Falls, New York, in 1848, Douglass supported the controversial demand for women's suffrage—the right to vote. What was the point of having the right to vote, however, if women did not use it? Even if, as the Garrisonians preached, the Constitution was evil, it did not follow that participation in politics also was evil. Douglass began to rethink some of Garrison's positions.

In 1848, some antislavery members of the Democratic Party (known as "Barnburners") joined with antislavery members of the Whig Party ("Conscience" Whigs) and the remnants of the abolitionist Liberty Party to organize a new political party. Douglass attended the convention in Buffalo, New York, that led to the founding of the Free-Soil Party. The party's platform was to keep slavery out of the territory acquired from Mexico in the Mexican-American War of 1846–1848. The Free-Soil Party nominated former president Martin Van Buren for president in 1848. Van Buren gained 291,000 votes, more than 10 percent of the national total.

The Free-Soil Party avoided any talk of abolition. Members tried not to discuss the morality of slavery. Instead, the party attacked a "slave power conspiracy" composed of southern planters and northern business owners. Free-Soilers complained that this slave power conspiracy threatened American freedom for white people. Free-Soilers wanted the American West to remain "free soil" to be worked by "free (white) labor." William Lloyd Garrison made fun of the new party; he mocked its platform as "white manism." This new party's appeal widened the popularity of antislavery, however. The Free-Soil Party turned white racists in the North into antislavery voters.

All of this fascinated Douglass. He realized that the Free-Soil Party had its faults. Yet he still supported it. In 1849, he wrote that the party had "rallied a large number of people of the North in apparent hostility to the whole system of American slavery." The Free-Soil Party served as the bridge that led Northern voters, in the 1850s, from the strongly abolitionist and unpopular Liberty Party to the new (and, in the North, widely popular) Republican Party. Douglass did not convert overnight to a belief in using politics against slavery. He was slowly drifting away from the Garrisonians, however.

THE DECLARATION OF SENTIMENTS

The burned-over district was not only an abolitionist haven. In 1848, when the revolutionary Women's Rights Convention met in Seneca Falls, Douglass made the short trip from Rochester to attend the convention.

The women's conference had an abolitionist origin. In 1840, Americans Lucretia Mott and Elizabeth Cady Stanton had gone to the World Anti-Slavery Convention in London. Even though the two women were official delegates, they were refused permission to speak and forced to sit in the balcony. Mott and Stanton were enraged. They vowed to organize a women's rights convention. After eight years of struggle, they called together the convention at Seneca Falls, Stanton's hometown.

In the United States, because women could not vote, they suffered taxation without representation. American women could not become lawyers or doctors. Most American colleges would not accept women. Churches prevented women from becoming ministers, even though women were the majority of churchgoers. Marriage and divorce laws favored men. The women who met at Seneca Falls protested against these inequalities.

At the first session, Stanton presented the delegates with a Declaration of Sentiments. This statement, written mainly by Stanton, was modeled after the American Declaration of Independence. It proclaimed, "All men and women are created equal." The delegates unanimously passed resolutions demanding

A longtime supporter of women's rights, Douglass wrote articles in his newspaper, the *North Star*, in favor of women having the right to vote. Elizabeth Cady Stanton, one of the most famous activists in U.S. history, developed a friendship with Douglass and invited him to attend the first women's rights convention in Seneca Falls, New York.

expanded educational and professional opportunities for women and fairer laws for marriage and divorce. The final Declaration of Sentiments was signed by 68 women and 32 men.

The only demand that received any opposition at Seneca Falls was Stanton's call for women's suffrage. Many women feared that such a radical request would make them look ridiculous. Despite these fears, the convention narrowly supported Stanton's demand for women's right to vote. The measure passed, in part, because of the backing provided by Douglass.

Douglass always had been a strong supporter of women's rights. The slogan on the masthead of the *North Star* read, "Right is of No Sex, Truth is of No Color." Douglass attended and spoke at many women's rights conventions. Elizabeth Cady Stanton called him the only man who really understood what it felt like to be disenfranchised. Douglass empathized with the frustration of the talented women who could not sit downstairs at public meetings or speak to audiences that contained men.

Douglass wrote about the Seneca Falls convention in the *North Star*. He praised the Declaration of Sentiments and stated that, "In respect to political rights, we hold women to be justly entitled to all we claim for man. . . . All political rights which it is expedient for man to exercise, it is equally so for women." Douglass was always proud of his participation in the women's movement. "When I ran away from slavery, it was for myself," he said. "When I advocated emancipation, it was for my people; but when I stood up for the rights of women, self was out of the question, and I found a little nobility in the act."

A Turbulent
Decade

After the Mexican-American War of 1846–1848, the United States gained control over Texas and the territory that later became California, New Mexico, Nevada, Utah, and parts of Colorado and Arizona. These lands had been closed to slavery under Mexican law. Whether the U.S. Congress would allow slavery in these new territories became a major political issue in the 1850s.

Free-Soilers insisted that the national government should make slavery illegal in all of the territories gained from Mexico. Free-Soilers had few objections to slavery where it already existed, but they did not want to see it spread. White Southerners, on the other hand, refused to support California's admission as a free state unless the U.S. government guaranteed that slavery always would be legal. Debate in Congress was very bitter, and a civil war threatened to break out.

After winning a large amount of new territory from Mexico, the U.S. government drafted the Compromise of 1850, which included the Fugitive Slave Act—legislation declaring that civilians had to assist in recapturing runaway slaves without granting them the right to a trial. Above, two runaway slaves captured in Boston are returned to their masters under the Fugitive Slave Act.

A crisis was avoided when all sides agreed to the so-called Compromise of 1850. That deal allowed California to enter the United States as a free state. In exchange, Northerners agreed to support a strong fugitive slave law. This law required the police, even in Northern free states, to pursue, capture, and return runaway slaves to their owners in the South.

The Compromise of 1850 outraged antislavery groups. The law denied a suspected fugitive's right to a jury trial. Instead, special commissioners handled the cases. The accused fugitive had no right to a lawyer, no right to present evidence, and no right to cross-examine witnesses. In the decade of the 1850s, under the Fugitive Slave Act, 332 suspected fugitives were returned to the South, and only 11 were freed.

Across the North, people who cared nothing about the issue of slavery felt offended by this violation of states' rights. In response, most Northern states passed "personal liberty laws." These laws provided lawyers for accused "fugitives" and required a trial by jury. Many blacks and whites called for violent resistance to the Fugitive Slave Act. In some cases, Northern mobs rescued supposed fugitives and sent them to Canada.

DOUGLASS CHANGES HIS MIND

In 1843, Douglass had blasted Henry Highland Garnet's call for slave rebellions. Now, Douglass urged blacks to resist the Fugitive Slave Act by all possible means. In a defiant speech in October 1850, Douglass proclaimed that fugitive slaves should be "resolved to die rather than to go back."

In March 1852, Harriet Beecher Stowe's antislavery novel, *Uncle Tom's Cabin*, was published in Boston. By June, 14 steam presses ran day and night to produce enough copies to meet the astonishing demand. The book was the biggest bestseller of the nineteenth century. "Nothing could have better suited the humane requirements of the hour," Douglass later said. "Its effect was amazing, instantaneous, and universal." Douglass saw immediately that *Uncle Tom's Cabin* would create white sympathy for slaves and therefore help bring about social change.

Douglass' house in Rochester became a regular stopping place for fugitives on their way to Canada. His daughter later wrote that Douglass "enlarged his home where a suite of rooms could be made ready for those fleeing to Canada. . . . It was no unusual occurrence for mother to be called up at all hours of the night . . . to prepare supper for a hungry lot of fleeing humanity."

GERRIT SMITH AND THE CONSTITUTION

Few white American reformers gave as much energy and money to the cause of African Americans as did Gerrit Smith. Smith was a wealthy upstate New York land speculator and abolitionist. In 1846, Smith gave away vast tracts of land in northern New York to about 3,000 African Americans.

Smith also was a founder and leader of the antislavery Liberty Party. Unlike Garrison, Smith firmly believed that the Constitution was an antislavery text. Smith cited the Preamble to the Constitution, which stated that the main purpose of the document was to "secure the blessings of liberty" to all Americans. Because slavery denied these blessings to slaves, Smith reasoned, the institution of slavery contradicted the Constitution. He also noted that the Constitution never uses the word *slavery*. Therefore, according to Smith, the document could not be given a proslavery interpretation. In 1852, upstate New York voters elected Smith to the U.S. Congress as a member of the Free-Soil Party.

In the 1850s, Smith replaced Garrison as Douglass' most important mentor. Smith, who did not live far from Rochester, became good friends with Douglass and even donated money to the *North Star* at crucial moments. "You not only keep life in my paper but keep spirits in me," Douglass wrote to Smith. In 1855, Douglass dedicated his second autobiography to Smith. Douglass said that the dedication was a "token of esteem for [Smith's] character, admiration for his genius and benevolence, affection for his person, and gratitude for his friendship."

As late as 1849, Douglass still called the Constitution "a most cunningly devised and wicked compact" that needed to be overthrown. In May 1851, Douglass announced in the *North Star* that he had changed his mind. He now declared that Smith was correct. The Constitution of the United States actually was a radical antislavery document to "be wielded in behalf of emancipation." Douglass argued that every American should use "his political as well as his moral power" to overthrow slavery.

In June 1851, Douglass merged the *North Star* with Gerrit Smith's *Liberty Party Paper*. The new paper was called *Frederick Douglass' Paper*. "There is no question," Douglass

Following a falling out with William Lloyd Garrison, Douglass found a new mentor in Gerrit Smith, a fellow abolitionist. Smith provided guidance and financial assistance to Douglass' work against slavery.

said, "that the antislavery movement will always be followed to a greater or lesser distance by a political party of some sort. It is inevitable."

THE FINAL SPLIT WITH GARRISON

Douglass claimed that, during his early speaking career, the Boston abolitionists had usually introduced him "as a 'chattel'—a 'thing'—a piece of Southern property—the chairman assuring the audience that it could speak." The Garrisonians tried to restrict Douglass to a simple narrative. "Give us the facts," said one abolitionist, and "we will take care of the philosophy." To introduce Douglass, William Lloyd Garrison said, "Tell your story, Frederick."

Douglass usually obliged. As late as 1846, on tour with Garrison, he told a British audience, "I feel that my friend Garrison is better able to instruct you." With Garrison sitting right there, Douglass said, "I never had a day's schooling in my life. . . . I come here to tell a simple tale of slavery, as coming under my own observation." He repeated similar statements even after Garrison returned to America.

By 1850, Douglass wanted to do more than just narrate the horrors of slavery. He wanted to denounce them. Douglass admitted that the Boston abolitionists were "excellent friends . . . actuated by the best of motives." Yet, he added, "Still I must speak just the word that seemed to me the word to be spoken by me."

During the early 1850s, Garrison first treated Douglass like a rebellious son and then like an ungrateful inferior. Douglass could not tolerate Garrison's inability to respect his decisions. He wanted Garrison to treat him as an equal. When Douglass decided to support the Free-Soil Party and wrote that the Constitution was an antislavery document, the Boston abolitionists branded him a traitor.

The Garrisonians felt that they had the only true way to fight slavery. Garrison removed the *North Star* from the AASS's list of approved newspapers. Several Boston abolitionists began to attack Douglass. This fighting among reformers angered Harriet Beecher Stowe. "Where is this work of excommunication to end?" she asked. "Is there but one true anti-slavery church and all the others infidels?"

In early 1855, Gerrit Smith helped to found the American Abolition Society. This organization was based on the principle of "the illegality and unconstitutionality of American slavery." Douglass joined Smith's new group, thereby completing his break from the Boston abolitionists. "When I escaped from slavery, and was introduced to the Garrisonians, I adopted very many of their opinions, and defended them just as long as I deemed them to be true," Douglass wrote. "Subsequent experience and reading have led me to . . . other conclusions. When I was a child, I thought and spoke as a child."

Despite their differences in opinion, Douglass always admired Garrison. In later life, Douglass kept a fine drawing of the editor of *The Liberator* in his library. He always admitted he owed a deep emotional and professional debt to Garrison.

WHAT, TO THE SLAVE, IS THE FOURTH OF JULY?

In 1852, the Rochester Ladies' Anti-Slavery Society invited the 34-year-old Douglass to give a speech in Rochester on Independence Day. Douglass insisted on speaking on July 5 rather than on July 4. This was the tradition in the black communities of New York. Nearly 600 people paid the twelve-and-a-half cents' admission to hear Douglass' long speech. In it, he cast himself in the role of an excluded victim bitterly demanding admission as an equal member to American society. Below is an excerpt from the speech that many consider the greatest antislavery oration ever delivered.

I am not included within the pale of this glorious anniversary! Your high independence only reveals the immeasurable distance between us. The blessings in which you, this day, rejoice, are not enjoyed in common. The rich inheritance of justice, liberty, prosperity, and independence, bequeathed by your fathers, is shared by you, not by me. The sunlight that brought life and healing to you has brought stripes and death to me. This Fourth [of] July is yours, not mine. You may rejoice, I must mourn. To drag a man in fetters into the grand illuminated temple of liberty, and call upon him to join you in joyous anthems, were inhuman mockery and sacrilegious irony. . . .

What, to the American slave, is your Fourth of July? I answer: a day that reveals to him, more than all other days in the year, the gross injustice and cruelty to which he is the constant victim. To him, your celebration is a sham; your boasted liberty, an unholy license; your national greatness, swelling vanity; your sounds of rejoicing are empty and heartless; your denunciations of tyrants, brass fronted impudence; your shouts of liberty and equality, hollow mockery; your prayers and hymns, your sermons and thanksgivings, with all your religious parade, and solemnity, are, to him, mere bombast, fraud, deception, impiety, and hypocrisy—a thin veil to cover up crimes which would disgrace a nation of savages. There is not a nation on the earth guilty of practices, more shocking and bloody, than are the people of these United States, at this very hour. Go where you may, search where you will . . . for revolting barbarity and shameless hypocrisy, America reigns without a rival.

THE HEROIC SLAVE

In 1852, Julia Griffiths thought up a new fund-raising scheme for *Frederick Douglass' Paper*. She asked abolitionist celebrities to submit antislavery statements with a copy of the author's signature at the bottom. The Rochester Ladies' Anti-Slavery Society published these short pieces the next year in a book called *Autographs for Freedom*. William Seward, Harriet Beecher Stowe, and Lewis Tappan all contributed antislavery essays. The book sold so well that a second edition was prepared the following year.

Most of the entries, such as a poem by John Greenleaf Whittier, were brief. Douglass' contribution, however, was a 65-page story entitled "The Heroic Slave." The short novel was Douglass' only attempt at writing fiction.

"The Heroic Slave" was a work of historical fiction. It told the story of a courageous slave who led a revolt aboard a slave ship in 1841. Douglass modeled the hero of the story, Madison Washington, after himself. When the story begins, Washington is a slave. He escapes but is recaptured as he tries to free his wife. He is sent by ship to New Orleans but leads a shipboard slave revolt along the way. The ship's captain and the slave owners are killed. Washington eventually steers the ship to the British West Indies. When he is accused of the white people's deaths, he declares, "I am not a murderer. . . . Liberty . . . is the motive of this night's work." Madison Washington speaks so persuasively that he is not returned to slavery in the United States.

In a sense, "The Heroic Slave" was Douglass' own autograph for freedom. In this short novel, he declared his independence from the Boston abolitionists. The novel's message is that black people are responsible for their own liberation. White people can be sympathetic and even helpful, but the active revolutionary with black skin is still the hero. Douglass identified himself with his rebel-hero.

MY BONDAGE AND MY FREEDOM

In 1855, Douglass had lived in the North for 17 years. In that year, he published his second autobiography, *My Bondage and My Freedom*. In this new book, Douglass expanded his account of the years he spent in freedom from the *Narrative*'s few paragraphs to more than 70 pages. Douglass carefully reworded and extended some of the stories of his Maryland years. These changes reveal how Douglass altered his interpretation of his past over the years.

My Bondage was a great success. The first printing of 5,000 copies sold out in two days. In a month, the second printing

THE ROCHESTER LADIES' ANTI-SLAVERY SOCIETY

In the summer of 1851, six women formally organized themselves into the Rochester Ladies' Anti-Slavery Society. They elected Susan Farley Porter as president and Julia Griffiths as secretary. "Slavery," according to the group's constitution, "is an evil that ought not to exist, and is a violation of the inalienable rights of man."

By 1852, the society had grown to 19 members. That year, the women held the first of their annual antislavery bazaars. These events raised money through the sale of items made locally or contributed by other antislavery societies. The Rochester society also sponsored lectures by Frederick Douglass, Gerrit Smith, and other abolitionists at Corinthian Hall in Rochester.

The society used most of the money it raised to support *Frederick Douglass' Paper*. The society had money left over to sponsor a school for free blacks in Kansas and to distribute antislavery materials in Kentucky. The women also participated in the Underground Railroad. The society's annual reports for 1855 and 1856 listed 136 fugitives who had passed through Rochester with the society's help.

The Rochester Ladies' Anti-Slavery Society continued its work during the Civil War. The women in Rochester were helped by the fund-raising of Griffiths, who by then was married and living in England. The Rochester women assisted escaped slaves who made their way to the Union lines. After the Civil War, however, the society could not find enough support for its efforts in freedmen's education. The Rochester Ladies' Anti-Slavery Society disbanded in 1868.

of 5,000 also sold out. The book was reprinted in 1856 and again in 1857. In total, it sold about 18,000 copies. Although *My Bondage and My Freedom* is not as famous as the *Narrative*, most critics now consider it the strongest of Douglass' three autobiographies.

In *My Bondage and My Freedom*, Douglass took back none of his praise for Garrison. He did, however, replace the introductory letters from Garrison and Wendell Phillips with a long introduction by James McCune, a brilliant black doctor and abolitionist. He also included a 58-page appendix that offered excerpts from his speeches.

The second autobiography is not just an updating of the first. In *My Bondage*, Douglass rethinks many of his positions. At the conclusion, Douglass states that he will no longer slavishly follow Garrison. As Douglass notes in the book, "I was growing and needed room." For Douglass, the ability to speak and think freely was crucial to his ability to grow as an individual. *My Bondage and My Freedom* lacks the triumphant ending of the earlier work. Instead, Douglass' second autobiography is an open-ended story of a continual struggle to be free.

THE *DRED SCOTT* DECISION AND EMIGRATIONISM

In 1857, the U.S. Supreme Court decided the famous case of *Dred Scott v. Sanford*. In its decision, the court stated that Congress could not declare slavery illegal because a slave was a form of property, and property is protected by the Constitution. The Supreme Court also ruled that black people, even if they were free, could never be citizens of the United States. The decision stated that blacks were "so far inferior, that they had no rights which a white man was bound to respect."

The *Dred Scott* decision is often considered the worst ruling ever made by the U.S. Supreme Court. An outraged Douglass called it an "infamous decision" and a "brazen misstatement of the facts of history." Douglass redoubled his efforts to work through politics to attack slavery. "Whereas pro-slavery men have . . . given the Constitution a pro-slavery interpretation against its plain reading," he declared, "let our votes put men into that Supreme Court who will decide . . . the Constitution is not [pro]-slavery."

The *Dred Scott* decision contributed to overturning the compromises between the North and the South that had existed for years. The ruling seemed to confirm every abolitionist charge against the slave power conspiracy. The Supreme Court looked like it was making it impossible to prohibit slavery anywhere.

Abolitionists felt thoroughly defeated. "Step by step we have seen the slave power advancing," wrote Douglass in 1857, "poisoning, corrupting, and perverting the institutions of the country." Twenty years of preaching about the sins of slavery had not brought emancipation. Instead, there had been an increase of half a million slaves, the enactment of a punitive Fugitive Slave Act, and the *Dred Scott* decision. The area of slave states continued to expand.

For many African Americans, the *Dred Scott* decision was the last straw. Emigrationists such as Martin Delany and Henry Highland Garnet began to attract serious attention in the free black communities of the North. If blacks could never be citizens or have civil rights in the United States, then what was the point in staying?

Douglass hated the idea of emigrationism. He considered it identical to white racist colonization schemes. He said, "We live here—have lived here—have a right to live here, and mean to live here." Douglass opposed the starting premise of emigrationism—that racial prejudice was permanent and racial equality impossible. Sometimes, Douglass attacked Delany and Garnet in his newspaper. Usually, he just ignored them.

Despite the setbacks of the 1850s, Douglass continued to believe that blacks had a future in America. "We should not as an oppressed people grow despondent," Douglass wrote. "Let us rejoice in hope."

ABOLITIONISTS ACCEPT VIOLENCE

Many black and some white abolitionists always had regarded violence as a way to end slavery. Didn't the Declaration of Independence state that an oppressed people could use force to gain their freedom if no other means were available?

Some people thought so. In 1829, David Walker, a free black Bostonian, published an appeal for the violent overthrow of slavery. Two years later, Nat Turner, a Virginia slave, led the largest slave revolt in U.S. history. Turner and Walker were heroes to many African Americans. Even nonviolent abolitionists admired black liberators such as Haiti's Toussaint L'Ouverture and Joseph Cinque, an enslaved West African who led a revolt aboard the slave ship *Amistad.*

After the passage of the Fugitive Slave Act, abolitionists began to take a more flexible position on the use of violence. Antislavery activists of both races defied the hated law. They led dramatic rescues of accused fugitive slaves in Boston, Massachusetts (1851); Syracuse, New York (1851); Christiana, Pennsylvania (1852); Boston, Massachusetts again (1854); and Oberlin, Ohio (1858). "Talk! Talk! Talk! That will never free the slaves," abolitionist John Brown complained. "What is needed is action—action." By the late 1850s, abolitionists such as Garrison, who continued to insist on nonviolence, were in the minority.

Douglass had never been a real pacifist, even when he followed Garrison. Douglass took pride in having fought Edward Covey. He doubted the effectiveness of Garrison's tactic of "moral persuasion" as a weapon for slaves. Douglass' arguments against violence were usually practical: The white masters had the guns, and the black slaves who fought against them would be killed. He wrote, "I never see much use in fighting, unless there is a reasonable probability of whipping somebody."

The Fugitive Slave Act pushed Douglass further from non-violence. Now he justified, and even celebrated, violence in self-defense against slave catchers. He declared that the "only way to make the Fugitive Slave Act a dead letter is to make half a dozen or more dead kidnappers." In his speeches in the 1850s, Douglass praised the white American heroes of the Revolution. He declared that black slave violence against white oppressors was just another way to fight for freedom. In "The Heroic Slave," Douglass has the slaves use their own broken chains to kill the captain of the slave ship and the slave owner.

DOUGLASS AND JOHN BROWN

Douglass probably began his long friendship with John Brown, the white abolitionist, in late 1847. The two men met when Douglass visited Brown's meager home in Springfield, Massachusetts. "The most interesting part of my visit to Springfield was a private interview with Mr. Brown," Douglass wrote in the *North Star*. "Though a white gentleman, [Brown] is in sympathy, a black man, and is as deeply interested in our cause, as though his own soul had been pierced with the iron of slavery." Douglass was impressed that Brown "thought that slaveholders had forfeited their right to live." He later recalled, "Our relations were friendly and confidential. I never passed through Springfield without calling on him, and he never came to Rochester without calling on me."

In January 1858, Brown visited Douglass in Rochester and stayed at his house for almost a month. Brown tried to persuade Douglass to support his plan to invade the South and wage a guerilla war against slavery from the Appalachian Mountains. While a guest at Douglass' house, Brown crafted a document that he grandly named "Provisional Constitution and Ordinance for the People of the United States." In this amazing document, Brown described a government and a set of laws for a new free state that he hoped to create in the area of his invasion.

Engraved by J.C.Buttre, New York.

A radical abolitionist, John Brown asked for Frederick Douglass' support for his raid on Harpers Ferry. The attack was meant to initiate an insurrection against the federal government and to establish a new, free territory within the United States. Douglass declined to participate in the raid, believing it would be detrimental to the antislavery movement.

In August 1859, just before Brown set out to attack Harpers Ferry, Virginia, he tried to convince Douglass to fight at his side. The two men met at an abandoned stone quarry outside Chambersburg, Pennsylvania. Brown described the planned raid in detail. He was dismayed when Douglass told him, "It's a perfect steel trap, John."

"Come with me, Douglass," Brown begged. "When I strike, the bees will begin to swarm, and I shall want you to help hive them." Douglass opposed Brown's plan "with all the arguments at my command. . . . It would be an attack on the Federal Government, and would array the whole country against us." For two days, Brown continued to attempt to persuade Douglass to join his force, but Douglass refused. It was the last time Douglass saw his old friend. Brown's October raid on Harpers Ferry failed, and Brown was executed in Virginia in December. Douglass later wrote of Brown, "His zeal in the cause of freedom was infinitely superior to mine. . . . I could live for the slave; John Brown could die for him."

Douglass was lecturing in Philadelphia when Brown's raid on Harpers Ferry took place. Douglass was in real danger. He was associated with Brown, and he knew about the raid. Virginia authorities charged Douglass with murder, robbery, and inciting a slave rebellion. A trial in Virginia almost certainly would have led to Douglass' execution. He quickly returned to Rochester and destroyed all papers connecting him to Brown. He then fled to Canada, just ahead of his pursuers. From Canada, Douglass went to England, where he already had scheduled a lecture tour.

Douglass never forgot his friendship with Brown. After the Civil War, Douglass wrote, "To have been acquainted with John Brown, shared his counsels, enjoyed his confidence, sympathized with the great objects in his life and death, I esteem as among the highest privileges of my life."

Recruiting
for Freedom

Douglass cut short his lecture tour of England when he heard that his daughter Annie had died on March 13, 1860. She was Frederick and Anna's youngest child and was not quite 11 years old. She had been ill since December. Douglass felt guilty that he had not been home for her sickness. He decided to return immediately to the United States.

Fortunately for Douglass, the prosecution of John Brown's supporters had been quietly dropped. Instead, everyone in America was hypnotized by the presidential campaign of 1860. For a few months, Douglass dealt with the pain of Annie's death. He also resumed publication of his newspaper and tried to decide whom to support for president. At first, he backed the tiny Radical Abolitionist Party, which was running Gerrit Smith for president. He hoped that the Republicans would win, but he wrote, "I cannot support Lincoln." By August, however, he was publicly supporting Abraham Lincoln for president.

THE REPUBLICAN PARTY

The Republican Party had replaced the Whig Party in 1854, after the passage of the Kansas-Nebraska Act. The Republican Party was a sectional party that drew all of its strength from the North. Republicans usually were not abolitionists. Most Republicans, such as Lincoln, believed that the Constitution protected slavery in the South, where it already existed. They were totally opposed to any expansion of slavery into the American West, however.

Between 1856 and the Civil War, Douglass usually supported the Republican Party. He admitted that the party was too conservative, however, because "while it battles against the spread of slavery . . . [it] admits its right to exist anywhere." He hated the fact that the Republican Party did not judge slavery to be immoral and evil. "[T]he Republican Party is far from an abolition party," Douglass wrote, but "I cannot fail to see also that [it] carries with it the antislavery sentiment of the North, and that a victory gained by it . . . will be a victory gained . . . over the wickedly aggressive pro-slavery sentiment of the country."

The Republicans felt that they could win the presidential election of 1860. In an attempt to do this, they did not nominate William Seward, the controversial abolitionist from New York. Instead, they chose the more moderate Abraham Lincoln of Illinois. Lincoln's main opponent was Stephen A. Douglas, a Democratic senator from Illinois. The Democrats tried to paint Lincoln as a crazy radical abolitionist. They did this by linking Douglass' name with the Republican Party as often as they could.

The Republicans wanted to win the election. They tried to distance themselves from Douglass and from any issues of black equality. The Republican strategy was successful. In 1860, Lincoln was elected president of the United States. He won a four-person race with about 40 percent of the vote. Lincoln won every Northern state except New Jersey.

THE CIVIL WAR BEGINS

As a Republican, President Lincoln believed that slavery should not expand to the West. In 1861, in his inaugural address, he promised the white South, "I have no purpose, directly or indirectly, to interfere with the institution of slavery in the States where it exists. I believe I have no lawful right to do so, and I have no inclination to do so."

Douglass was outraged by this speech. He showed no sympathy for the president's difficult position in the face of the threat of Southern secession. Douglass bitterly claimed that Lincoln had sunk to "the same moral level" as slaveholders.

In contrast to Douglass, 11 Southern states did not believe Lincoln's words. These states decided to leave the United States and form their own country, the Confederate States of America. The American Civil War began in April 1861, when Southern rebels attacked Fort Sumter, a U.S. fort outside Charleston, South Carolina.

Douglass saw the Civil War as an opportunity to destroy slavery forever. After the *Dred Scott* decision, the future had seemed hopeless. Now, it was filled with excitement and possibility. Douglass said that "the bloodiest war is preferable to the so-called peace that we 'enjoyed' under the rule of Democrats and slaveholders." For Douglass, the Civil War was a contest between good and evil. "From the first," he wrote, "I saw in this war the end of slavery and truth requires me to say that my interest in the success of the North was largely due to this belief."

Throughout the Civil War, Douglass feared that the North would compromise with the South. Such a compromise would

The differences between North and South became serious when Southern rebels attacked Fort Sumter *(above)* in South Carolina, signaling the start of the American Civil War. Because slavery was a commonly argued subject between the North and South, many viewed the Civil War as a fight for the freedom of all people.

preserve sectional harmony at the expense of black freedom. Douglass hated compromise. He demanded the immediate abolition of slavery, the enlistment of black troops, and a guarantee of equal rights. "Not a slave should be left a slave in the returning footprints of the American army gone to put down this slaveholding rebellion," declared Douglass in June 1861. "Sound policy, not less than humanity, demands the liberation of every slave in the rebel states."

After Fort Sumter, Douglass worked hard to support the Union effort in the war. He wrote and spoke to inspire hatred of the slaveholding planters and the whole white South. "What is a slaveholder but a rebel and a traitor?" he asked. A slaveholders' rebellion, Douglass believed, could be defeated only by destroying slavery.

THE EMANCIPATION PROCLAMATION

The problem of slavery was a direct cause of the Civil War. During the first two years of the war, however, President Lincoln tried to ignore the problem. Slavery still was legal in the border states of Maryland, Kentucky, Missouri, and Delaware. To keep these border states in the Union, Lincoln insisted that the war was not about slavery but about preserving the Union.

Douglass constantly pressed Lincoln and everyone in Washington to turn the war into an antislavery crusade. Douglass complained that the border states were a "millstone about the neck of the government." In a speech entitled "Fighting the Rebels with One Hand," he argued that, "We are striking the guilty rebels with our soft, white hand, when we should be striking with the iron hand of the black man, which we keep chained behind us. We have been catching slaves instead of arming them."

Douglass was annoyed with President Lincoln's refusal to make emancipation the aim of the Civil War. In August 1862, Douglass unleashed a bitter attack on the president. He declared that every move Lincoln had made "had been calculated in a marked and decided way to shield and protect slavery."

In September 1862, after the bloody battle of Antietam, Lincoln issued a preliminary Emancipation Proclamation. This order gave the Confederate states 100 days to give up the war without losing their slaves. Lincoln received no response. On January 1, 1863, Lincoln declared that all slaves in areas under Confederate control were now free. In this final Emancipation Proclamation, Lincoln added a provision that allowed the enlistment of blacks in the U.S. Army for the first time in more than 50 years.

The Emancipation Proclamation dramatically affected the Civil War. It committed the Union to the abolition of slavery as an objective of the war. Under the proclamation, slavery would be ended by force as the Union Army marched through the South. Emancipation would be immediate. Slaveholders would not receive any compensation for their freed slaves.

Douglass was thrilled. He rightly believed that the Emancipation Proclamation meant "the entire abolition of slavery, wherever the evil could be reached by the federal arm, and I saw that its moral power would extend much further." Lincoln may have been a cautious man, but he reached an amazingly radical conclusion. Only 18 months before he issued his preliminary proclamation, the president had promised not to interfere with slavery in the Southern states. "We are all liberated by this proclamation," Douglass said in February 1863. "It is a mighty event for the bondman, but it is a still mightier event for the nation at large."

FORT WAGNER

Douglass never thought that the end of slavery was enough for African Americans. As soon as the Emancipation Proclamation was issued, he had a new goal. He wanted to press the U.S. government to enlist black men into the U.S. Army and U.S. Navy.

African Americans had fought in all of the nation's major wars. Despite this, the Union officially excluded black soldiers from the army for the first 18 months after Fort Sumter. This policy enraged Douglass. He called it a "spectacle of blind, unreasoning prejudice." He insisted that blacks were loyal Americans who would fight as strongly for the Union as they would fight against the slaveholding Confederacy.

Shortly after the final Emancipation Proclamation, the governor of Massachusetts called for black volunteers for the famous 54th Massachusetts Volunteers infantry regiment. Black men often were reluctant to fight in a white man's army, however. Douglass decided to help the recruiting effort. His famous call for volunteers, "Men of Color to Arms," appeared in the March 1863 issue of one of his publications, *Douglass' Monthly*. In this call, Douglass urged blacks to "end in a day the bondage of centuries" and to earn their equality by fighting for the Union. "Action! Action! Not criticism, is the plain duty of this hour," Douglass proclaimed. "Liberty won by white men would lose half its luster. Who would be free themselves must strike the blow. Better even to die free, than to live slaves."

Douglass traveled widely across upstate New York to encourage black men to enlist. He signed up more than 100 men from New York State for the 54th Massachusetts Volunteers, including his sons Charles and Lewis. Many other black leaders supported the recruiting effort, including former emigrationists Martin Delany and Henry Highland Garnet.

Douglass knew that many white Americans would not welcome black soldiers. "Colored men going into the army and the navy of the United States must expect annoyance," Douglass warned. "They will be severely criticized and even insulted—but let no man hold back on this account. . . . A half a loaf is better than no bread—and going into the army is the speediest way to overcome the prejudice that has dictated unjust laws against us."

The 54th Massachusetts left Boston for South Carolina in May 1863. The regiment was ordered to attack Fort Wagner, an artillery post that guarded Charleston harbor. On July 18, the black soldiers directly assaulted the front of the fort. The attackers made it as far as the walls before the Confederates

The 54th Massachusetts Volunteer Infantry was one of the first major American military units made up of black soldiers (except for the officers). The 54th attacked Fort Wagner on July 18, 1863. Although the Union suffered massive casualties, the battle was a political victory for the Union since the bravery of the all-black unit against insurmountable odds proved the worth of black soldiers and spurred additional recruitment to the Union Army. The battle has been depicted in this painting called *The Storming of Ft. Wagner* and in the 1989 film *Glory*.

drove them back in vicious hand-to-hand fighting. Lewis Douglass wrote, "Men fell all around me. A shell would explode and clear a space of twenty feet, our men would close up again, but it was no use we had to retreat, which was a very hazardous undertaking. How I got out of that fight alive I cannot tell, but I am here."

At the battle of Fort Wagner, 174 Confederate defenders were killed or wounded. In comparison, there were 1,515

Union casualties. The valor displayed in this battle by black soldiers ended any attempts to keep them out of fighting positions in the army. In the last two years of the war, nearly 200,000 blacks (about 80 percent of them former slaves) joined the Union Army and Navy. This figure represented about 10 percent of all Union soldiers. The participation of black soldiers was one of the most revolutionary features of the Civil War. In 1860, almost no one expected to see thousands of former slaves marching through the South to do battle with their ex-masters.

MEETINGS WITH PRESIDENT LINCOLN

Even after Fort Wagner, black soldiers often were treated badly. They received only $10 per month in pay, as compared with the $13 per month paid to white soldiers. Black soldiers who were taken prisoner by the Confederates were not treated like white soldiers. The Confederate Congress declared in May 1863 that it was acceptable to execute black men with guns because they were rebellious slaves. Douglass and many others denounced this racist policy. As a result, Lincoln signed an order in July requiring that "for every soldier of the United States killed in violation of the laws of war, a rebel soldier shall be executed."

In August 1863, Douglass was invited to the White House to meet with President Lincoln. Douglass thanked the president for his July 1863 retaliation order. Douglass then raised the issue of equal pay for all soldiers. Lincoln responded frankly and respectfully and denied being either hesitant or cowardly. The president defended his policies and the pace of change regarding the slavery question. Lincoln reminded Douglass that the president had to lead the people without getting too far ahead of popular opinion.

Douglass was not sure what to make of Lincoln. At one point during the war, Douglass baldly declared, "Mr. Lincoln is quite a genuine representative of American prejudice and negro hatred." Yet Lincoln also charmed Douglass. "Though I was not entirely satisfied with his views," Douglass remembered, "I was so well satisfied with the man and with the educating tendency of the conflict that I determined to go on with recruiting." Douglass was impressed with Lincoln's patience and sincerity. He returned to Rochester and toned down his public criticism of the president. In some private letters, however, Douglass still denounced Lincoln in vicious terms. Not until June 1864 did Congress authorize equal pay for black and white troops.

Lincoln invited Douglass to the White House for another meeting in August 1864. Douglass was amazed at how much he felt at ease in Lincoln's presence. "In his company," he said, "I was never in any way reminded of my humble origin, or my unpopular color." Douglass hoped that Lincoln would appoint him as the first black officer in the U.S. Army. The commission never came through. Instead, the honor went to Douglass' old friend and rival, Martin Delany.

Lincoln was careful and deliberate; Douglass was quick and impulsive. It took 18 months for Lincoln to proclaim emancipation. In Douglass' mind, this was too long. It also took Douglass a long time to understand the problems that existed for an antislavery president. After the Civil War ended, Douglass decided that he had perhaps judged Lincoln too quickly. He noted that, from the abolitionist point of view, "Lincoln seemed tardy, cold, dull, and indifferent." Lincoln was president, however, and as such, he had to be measured "by the sentiment of his country." By that standard, Douglass admitted that Lincoln was "swift, zealous, radical and determined."

THE END OF THE CIVIL WAR

In February 1864, Douglass explained "his idea for the mission of the war." For African Americans, said Douglass, the Civil War should result in "liberty for all, chains for none;

the black man a soldier in war; a laborer in peace; a voter in the South as well as the North; America his permanent home, and all Americans his fellow countrymen."

This was a revolutionary program that was far beyond what anyone could have imagined five years earlier. The Thirteenth Amendment to the U.S. Constitution, which was ratified in 1865, abolished and prohibited slavery. Thousands of black soldiers marched in the Union Army. Many former slave quarters were turned into schools. The U.S. government was willing to play a role in helping black people in the South. Some land distribution seemed a real possibility. Northern states repealed certain segregation laws. Douglass had good cause for optimism.

Yet Douglass also felt a little empty. When the Civil War ended, he wrote, "I felt that I had reached the end of the noblest and best part of my life. . . . The antislavery platform had performed its work, and my voice was no longer needed." Douglass had been an abolitionist since he first knew what the word meant. Now, at age 47, he had to decide how he wanted to shape his life in the years ahead.

Events forced Douglass' hand. He noted, "Though slavery was abolished, the wrongs of my people were not ended. Though they were not slaves, they were not yet quite free." Thousands of former slaves had fled from hated masters, had left farms and plantations that were ruined by the war, or had tried to reunite with their families. Black refugees needed food and shelter. Southern whites began passing laws called Black Codes. These laws attempted to return blacks to a condition of virtual slavery by taking away their rights and forcing them to work for their former masters. Once again, Douglass felt obligated to speak up for racial justice.

MEETING WITH PRESIDENT JOHNSON

Douglass was torn between two conflicting ideas. Sometimes he wanted the U.S. government to help the freed people. At

other times, he insisted that black people could rise immediately from the damage of slavery without help. Douglass
expected self-reliance from blacks, but he also demanded
justice from the nation.

Douglass did not count on President Andrew Johnson's
leniency toward the white South. Johnson, a Democrat from
the South, became president after Lincoln's assassination
in April 1865. Johnson was a racist who supported states'
rights and expressed hostility toward black civil and political
rights.

By the end of 1865, Douglass was disgusted with the situation for blacks in the South. His new passion was to gain the
vote for black people. He declared, "I can see little advantage
in emancipation without this." Douglass accurately predicted
that if freed black men did not win the ballot, they would
be in the absolute power of Southern whites. He wrote, "No
man can be truly free whose liberty is dependent upon the
thought, feeling, and action of others, and who has himself no
means in his own hands for guarding, protecting, defending,
and maintaining that liberty."

Douglass was part of a black delegation that met
with Johnson in February 1866. After Douglass spoke,
Johnson gave one of the most shockingly racist speeches
ever given by an American president. He told Douglass
that blacks who demanded the right to vote were ungrateful. Johnson declared that he would never support black
suffrage because it would lead to a race war in the South.
Instead, Johnson suggested to the delegation that leaving
the country was the best option for the freed people. The
president denounced Douglass as a dealer "in rhetoric . . .
who never periled life, liberty, or property."

Douglass was used to racial harassment. He never
expected to find such open prejudice in the White House,
however. After the departure of the black delegation, President
Johnson cursed out its members, especially Douglass.

Congress soon impeached Johnson and drove him from office. The Fourteenth Amendment to the Constitution, ratified in 1868, protected the rights of former slaves. The amendment declared that anyone born in the United States was a citizen. This overturned the *Dred Scott* decision. In addition, the Fourteenth Amendment stated that the Constitution's Bill of Rights applied to the states. It required states to provide equal protection under the law to everyone in the state, regardless of skin color.

THE FIFTEENTH AMENDMENT

Douglass traveled all over the United States to speak in support of black voting rights. "Slavery is not abolished until the black man has the ballot," Douglass told his audiences. The ability to vote would protect blacks in the South from white racism and hostility. In addition, any possible success for the Republican Party in the South depended on black voters. Douglass insisted that "the freedman should have the ballot . . . to guard, protect and maintain his liberty. . . . The liberties of the American people were dependent upon the ballot-box, the jury-box, and the cartridge-box—that without these no class of people could live and flourish in this country."

The Fifteenth Amendment to the Constitution barred states from denying the vote to any citizen based on race, color, or previous condition of servitude (slavery). The amendment was passed by Congress in March 1869 and ratified by the states in February 1870. Black citizens celebrated what they thought was the capstone of the revolution. Even Douglass was stunned. "I seem to myself to be living in a new world," he remarked about the Fifteenth Amendment. "The sun does not shine as it used to." The next month, the AASS disbanded; its leaders declared that its work was done. "We have a future," Douglass told a crowd in the central square of his old hometown of Baltimore. "Everything is possible to us."

Because of the Fifteenth Amendment, more blacks were elected to political office from 1865 to 1880 than at any other time in American history. Terrorist groups such as the Ku Klux Klan tried to intimidate black voters and white Republicans. Nevertheless, U.S. soldiers in the South supported democratically elected state governments. For Douglass, the passage of the Fifteenth Amendment meant "that color is no longer to be a calamity; that race is no longer a crime; and that liberty is to be the right of all."

THE RACIST COUNTERREVOLUTION

For a brief time, black men exercised citizenship rights in the South. The Union Army and the U.S. government helped them. By the 1870s, however, the bright new day for blacks in the South began to fade. White Southerners could adjust to the end of slavery, but they refused even to consider black social equality or black voting rights. Nor were Southern whites willing to give or sell land to free blacks who wanted to farm. Southern whites tried to keep their power over the former slaves.

Hooded nightriders burned, raped, and murdered black men and women. The Ku Klux Klan killed teachers for the crime of teaching black children. African Americans who dared to vote in the Deep South were assaulted or threatened. White law enforcement did not interfere and even cooperated with the violent racists. The Democratic Party began to reform itself in the South as a white man's party. The Republican Party in the South began to disappear.

At the same time, Northerners lost interest in the racial situation in the South. They ignored the attempts by Southern whites to reenslave the people who had been freed. Northerners wanted to forget the Civil War. They preferred to concentrate on new issues such as industrialization and urbanization.

During the 1870s, white Southerners stripped away black rights. One by one, the Southern states established white-only governments. They confined African Americans to agricultural labor and deprived them of their political rights. By 1900, black Southerners faced an entrenched, segregated system that was designed to keep them oppressed.

In 1872, Douglass' home in Rochester burned to the ground. None of his family was hurt, but many of his papers

THE SPLIT WITH THE WOMEN'S RIGHTS MOVEMENT

Ever since the 1848 Women's Rights Convention at Seneca Falls, the antislavery and women's rights movements had been closely associated. Many feminists had begun their reform careers as abolitionists. These women felt that if black men could vote, white women and black women also should be able to vote.

Unfortunately, the text of the Fifteenth Amendment did not support women's suffrage. It allowed states to deny the vote to women. Elizabeth Cady Stanton and Susan B. Anthony, both old friends of Frederick Douglass', broke with Republican abolitionists. Stanton and Anthony refused to support the Fifteenth Amendment. Anthony declared that she "would sooner cut off my right hand than ask the ballot for the black man and not for women." In 1869, Stanton and Anthony formed the National Woman Suffrage Association (NWSA). The organization supported a range of reforms for women, including better treatment in the courts and in workplaces. It also lobbied for women's suffrage by amendment to the U.S. Constitution.

were lost, including the only complete runs of all of his newspapers. Someone had set the fire intentionally, but no arsonist
was ever identified.

The destruction of the family house ended the 25 years of
Douglass' life in Rochester. Friends urged Douglass to rebuild
in upstate New York, but he turned his back on the burned-
over district. Instead, he moved to the center of political
activity: Washington, D.C.

Douglass always had supported women's rights. He had
argued for women's suffrage at the Seneca Falls convention. Now, however, he refused to back Stanton on this
issue. "While the negro is mobbed, beaten, shot, stabbed,
hanged, burnt, and is the target of all that is malignant in
the north and all that is murderous in the south, his claims
may be preferred by me," Douglass said. Many a woman
is the victim of abuse, "to be sure, but it cannot be pre-
tended I think that her cause is as urgent as . . . ours."
When someone asked Douglass whether black women were
not also assaulted in the South, Douglass responded that
black women were attacked because they were black and
not because they were women.

In 1869, former abolitionists Lucy Stone and Thomas
Higginson formed the American Woman Suffrage
Association (AWSA). This group focused only on women's
suffrage, to be achieved by state legislation. The AWSA
was more conservative than the NWSA. The AWSA tried to
keep an alliance with the Republican Party. Douglass supported the AWSA. For the next 21 years, the two suffrage
organizations competed for leadership of the women's
movement.

The Cedar Hill Years

From 1868 to 1876, Douglass loyally supported President Ulysses S. Grant and the Republican Party. Grant thought Douglass was too controversial to place in a high-ranking government job, however. Douglass received only a minor appointment as a member of the Santo Domingo Commission in 1871. Douglass surprised everyone by supporting the annexation of Santo Domingo (present-day Dominican Republic) to the United States.

Because he could not get a paid government job, Douglass decided to launch a weekly newspaper intended for "Colored America." The *New Era* began publishing in January 1870. Douglass soon became the primary editor of the paper, which was renamed the *New National Era*. "I have bought the entire printing establishment of the *New National Era*," he wrote to

Gerrit Smith, "and have given it to my three sons in the hope that they may be able to serve themselves as well as their people."

Douglass wanted the *New National Era* to be a model of black enterprise and self-improvement. To Douglass' disappointment, the plan failed. The paper never established a national reputation, and it folded in October 1874. Douglass claimed that he never regretted the investment of time and energy, although he lost about $10,000. "A misadventure though it was . . . I have no tears to shed. The journal was valuable while it lasted."

Douglass went back to his grueling career as a traveling lecturer. He was disappointed in his four children, who never seemed to be able to deal with the difficulties of racism in the United States. The four were in and out of jobs and depended on Douglass for financial support. The situation was grinding him down. He wrote to his daughter, "My long public career of traveling has cured my desire for a change of location."

THE FREEDMAN'S SAVINGS BANK

In early 1874, Douglass became president of the Freedman's Savings Bank. Congress had chartered the bank in 1865 as a safe place for African Americans to invest their money. The U.S. government's money did not back these black investors, however.

The Freedman's Bank opened branches across the country. Thousands of hardworking black people deposited more than $57 million in the bank. By 1874, however, the bank was on the verge of ruin because of bad management, speculation, incompetence, and fraud. Rumors circulated that the bank might fail. Many customers began to withdraw their savings. The trustees chose Douglass as president. He was a respected black American. His presence might inspire confidence in depositors and prevent the bank's collapse.

Douglass loved his fancy bank office, the prestige of the position, and the lack of travel involved in the job. It apparently never occurred to him that running a bank might require

Department of Justice, (Freedman's Bank Building.)

One of the disappointments in Douglass' life involved the Freedman's Savings Bank. Though he enjoyed his position at the bank, Douglass was not qualified to run the business, and his inexperience and lack of knowledge led to the ruin of many black people.

specialized skills. Douglass ignored the rumors that the bank was in trouble. By May, however, he knew that he had made a mistake. "I have got myself in a hard place in this Freedman's Bank," he wrote to his son-in-law, "and shall consider myself fortunate if I get out of it as easily as I got into it."

Only three months after Douglass' appointment, the Freedman's Bank failed. "I have neither taste nor talent for the place," he confessed. Thousands of black sharecroppers, laborers, and domestic workers lost their life savings. It was one of the more embarrassing moments in Douglass' career.

A STALWART REPUBLICAN

From 1872 until his death, Douglass supported the Republican Party. He considered it the only possible choice for black voters. In his speeches, he sometimes associated the Republican and Democratic parties with good and evil. "We are . . . entitled," he argued, "to call the Democratic Party a party of murder, robbery, treason, dishonesty, and fraud." He idealized the Republican Party as the power that "saved the nation, conquered the rebellion, put down the slaveholders' war, and liberated four million of bondmen." The rebirth of the Democratic Party infuriated him. "For the life of me," he wrote, "I cannot see how any honest colored man, who has brains enough to put two ideas together, can allow himself, under the notions of independence, to give aid and comfort to the Democratic Party."

The years of the late 1800s saw great economic and social changes in the United States. Faced with new problems, both the North and the South tried to forget about the Civil War. Old enemies embraced in a sectional reunion. Forgotten was the issue of rights of former slaves in the South. After 1876, the Republican Party lost its radical edge, and the party's idealism slipped away. Many Republican office holders settled into the corruption that comes with political power.

Douglass angrily resisted the desire of the country to forget the agony of the Civil War. Douglass' support for the Republican Party was a statement about the meaning of the war. If Northerners forgot the war, they also would forget black freedom in the South. Douglass reminded Americans that the South fought "to bind with chains millions of the human race." For Douglass, the Civil War always would be about emancipation. He did not really understand that most whites did not feel that way.

Douglass challenged the Republican Party to return to their antislavery tradition. Unfortunately, Republican leaders ignored his appeals. In 1879, Douglass said that the greatest mistake the Republicans ever made was to allow the "loyal North" to turn "away from the ghastly scene of war and the past," to "let bygones be bygones, to forgive and forget." Douglass did not want national unity without racial justice. He especially hated the praise heaped on the traitorous Southern general, Robert E. Lee. "There was a right side and a wrong side in the late war," Douglass thundered, "which no sentiment ought to cause us to forget. I say, if this war is to be forgotten, I ask, in the name of all things sacred, what shall men remember?"

GOVERNMENT POSITIONS

Douglass' loyalty to the Republican Party also was motivated by personal ambition. He hoped for a federal job equal to his reputation and in line with his support. The presidential election of 1876 was a close one. Douglass campaigned tirelessly for Rutherford B. Hayes among black voters in the North. When Hayes won, he appointed Douglass as marshal of Washington, D.C. Douglass accepted the ceremonial position gladly. The steady job in Washington finally allowed him, for the first time in 35 years, to cut down on his grueling lecture schedule.

Douglass soon realized that it was difficult to be both a black activist and a loyal Republican office holder. The cost of the government job was that he had to remain silent when President Hayes removed federal troops from the South. Between 1877 and 1881, African Americans in the South were under attack by whites. During those years, Douglass preached mostly about black self-improvement and progress.

In 1881, Republican James Garfield won the presidency and gave the marshal's job to a friend. Garfield appointed Douglass to the post of recorder of deeds for Washington, D.C. This was a step down for Douglass, but it was still steady employment. He held the position for five years, even into the first administration of President Grover Cleveland, a Democrat. The position had no social duties, and Douglass could speak as he wanted.

Douglass still seemed unwilling to confront issues with the directness he had showed in the 1850s, however. The Republican Party called on him whenever they needed to win black voters in the North. Douglass' government positions often helped him, and helped the Republican Party, more than they helped African Americans in general. Douglass abandoned his position as an angry outsider. Instead, he tried to work with white politicians to change things. "Government is better than anarchy, and patient reform is better than violent revolution," he said in 1883. This directly reversed his position in the late 1850s.

Douglass could not shake his allegiance to the Republican Party even as the party abandoned blacks. "I knew that however bad the Republican Party was, the Democratic Party was much worse," he said in 1891. "The Democratic Party was the party of reaction and the chosen party of the old master class."

SELF-MADE MEN

Throughout his career, Douglass appealed for black self-reliance. "The time has come," he declared in 1870, "for the colored men of the country to assume the duties and responsibilities of their own existence." Douglass had three or four set speeches that earned him about $6,000 in speaking fees each year. His talk entitled "Self-Made Men" was by far his most popular, however. He began giving it in the late 1850s, but it became his main moneymaker after the Civil War. The speech seemed to capture perfectly the national mood of the 1870s and 1880s. Douglass often selected this speech when he was asked to speak before black religious or educational bodies.

"Self-Made Men" celebrated people who rose from low birth to fame through their own courage and hard work. Douglass offered himself as an example, along with people such as

Abraham Lincoln, the Scottish poet Robert Burns, and Benjamin Banneker, the great black inventor and astronomer of the late 1700s. Douglass preached a strong work ethic, and he insisted that blacks should accumulate property. "We must not beg men

CEDAR HILL

In 1877, Frederick Douglass purchased his final home and named it Cedar Hill. The house was in Uniontown, an integrated community in the District of Columbia, across the Potomac River from the city of Washington, in the Anacostia Hills. He expanded the old house on the property from 14 to 21 rooms. He also purchased more land, to increase his holding to 24 acres. Cedar Hill had room for Douglass' library of 2,000 books and was big enough for him to entertain his many grandchildren.

Douglass' new residence was spacious and comfortable. The best thing about Cedar Hill, however, was its location. The house was perched high on a hilltop and had a spectacular view of the U.S. Capitol. The property had a fine garden, an orchard, and even a barn. Cedar Hill symbolized Douglass' triumph. In a sense, all of Washington, D.C., lay at his feet.

Douglass lived in this house until his death in 1895. His second wife, Helen Douglass, helped to preserve the house. The property was added to the U.S. National Park system in 1962. It was declared a National Historic Site in 1988.

The National Park Service now runs Cedar Hill. It is officially the Frederick Douglass National Historic Site, located at 1411 W. Street SE, in Anacostia. Almost all of the furnishings at Cedar Hill are original. Many of Douglass' personal possessions are on display. Cedar Hill still offers a sweeping view of the Capitol and the Washington, D.C., skyline.

to do for us what we ought to do for ourselves," he told both white and black audiences.

In the late 1870s, Douglass sometimes seemed out of touch with the lives of ordinary African Americans. By now, he had adopted a lifestyle that had little in common with the lives of most blacks, whether Northern or Southern, rural or urban. He did not like to be associated with illiterate black field workers. He was ashamed at the noise and the "shouting, singing, and stomping," that went on at many black gatherings. Douglass' personal success, his amazing intelligence, and his boundless energy made him impatient with the majority of people who could not follow in his footsteps.

Black people in America in the late nineteenth century faced vicious white violence and serious economic discrimination. Yet Douglass told farmhands and domestic servants on Maryland's Eastern Shore, "We must not talk about equality until we can do what the white people can do. As long as they can build vessels and we can not, we are their inferiors." White Americans liked this kind of speech, but most blacks saw its weaknesses. Hard work and temperance had limited value to people who had lost the right to vote and whose children had to pick cotton on land that they did not and could not own.

Douglass was not as out of touch as he seemed. It was just that the problems faced by America's black citizens were overwhelming. Douglass knew that the freedpeople were sent away empty-handed, without money, without friends, and without a foot of land to stand upon. He demanded justice and fair play from whites. He appealed to blacks for self-help and self-respect. Douglass knew, however, that without the support of the U.S. government, the future of black people in the South was bleak.

REMARRIAGE

In August 1882, Anna Murray Douglass died from a stroke. She was 69. She had been married to Frederick Douglass for 44 years. His wife's death sent Douglass into a severe depression.

Then, to everyone's surprise, in January 1884, he married Helen Pitts. The marriage set gossips talking. Douglass was a famous figure and a government official. Pitts was 20 years younger and white.

Pitts was born in Honeoye, New York, in 1838. She was the oldest daughter of parents with strong abolitionist and feminist beliefs. Pitts graduated from Mount Holyoke, a progressive women's seminary in Massachusetts, in 1857. She taught at the Hampton Institute, a Virginia college founded to serve black students. In 1880, Pitts moved in with her uncle in Washington, D.C. Her uncle was Douglass' neighbor at Cedar Hill. Pitts and Douglass had a common interest in women's

OTTILIE ASSING

In 1855, Julia Griffiths felt that her interracial friendship with Douglass was hurting the abolitionist cause, and she returned to England. Her absence left a void in Douglass' life that was filled by Ottilie Assing.

Assing was a German journalist and abolitionist. She was extremely well educated and worldly. Douglass and Assing first met in 1856, when Assing came to Rochester specifically to meet Douglass. She moved to Hoboken, New Jersey, where she wrote articles for German-American journals, sent back reports to German periodicals, and translated Douglass' *My Bondage and My Freedom* into German.

Assing was passionately in love with Douglass. The two were discreet but never secretive. For 26 years, Douglass was a frequent guest at Assing's home in Hoboken, and Assing spent all of her summers at the Douglass residences, first in Rochester and then in Washington, D.C. Douglass and

rights. In 1882, Douglass hired Pitts to work as a clerk in his recorder's office.

The marriage of Helen Pitts and Frederick Douglass caused great strain on both their families. Douglass' children were distressed with his marrying a white woman. Pitts' father, the former abolitionist, would not even allow Douglass to stay in his house.

Race mixing, or miscegenation, had long been one of white America's greatest fears. Many whites viewed interracial marriage as immoral, perverse, and a sin against nature. Douglass had no tolerance for this type of thinking. "What business has the world with the color of my wife?" he asked. Douglass com-

Assing walked arm in arm on the city streets, entertained friends together, worked together, and socialized together. She tutored his children and became like a second mother to them. When Douglass played the violin, Assing accompanied him on the piano. During the Civil War, she served with absolute loyalty as his ghostwriter, secretary, and confidante. The two were partners, and they may have been lovers, but they were not husband and wife.

Douglass never considered divorcing his wife. He felt loyal to Anna. He also knew that a divorce would wreck his career as a public leader. Assing saw herself as Douglass' natural wife, however. She was certain that Douglass eventually would marry her. After 28 years of loving support, she was disappointed. When Anna died, Douglass married a younger white woman, Helen Pitts. Six months after Douglass' remarriage, Assing committed suicide in Paris. In her will, she left most of her estate to Douglass.

plained that people "condemned me for marrying a wife a few shades lighter than myself. . . . In the popular eye, a shocking offense, and one for which I was to be ostracized by white and black alike."

Douglass' marriage angered many African Americans. They viewed interracial marriage, especially by a famous black man, as a betrayal of the race. "Goodbye, black blood in that family. We have no further use for him," wrote one black correspondent. "His picture hangs in our parlor; we will hang it in our stables."

In 1885 and 1887, Frederick and Helen toured Europe and North Africa. Together, they visited the grand sights of England, France, Italy, Greece, and Egypt. Douglass thoroughly enjoyed himself. His wife was unconventional, musical, intelligent, outspoken in her opinions, and full of laughter. Douglass was not attracted to the nineteenth-century ideal of the submissive wife. Instead, he liked women such as Julia Griffiths and Ottilie Assing—women who were well educated, independent, political, and witty. Throughout his life, Douglass looked to women as companions and sources of strength. He sensed that he could count on women, rather than men, to be competent and loyal.

THE LIFE AND TIMES OF FREDERICK DOUGLASS

Douglass' final autobiography, *The Life and Times of Frederick Douglass*, was published in 1881. Most people consider it the weakest of his three autobiographies. It lacked the passion of the *Narrative* or the analysis of *My Bondage and My Freedom*. Douglass reduced the space that he gave to his slavery experiences in order to tell about his Civil War and postwar activities.

The direct style of the *Narrative* was gone. *Life and Times* was a wordy account (more than 600 pages) of the life of a man of achievement. Douglass' theme was his rise to fame as a self-made man. He closed the book by praising "self-reliance, self-respect, industry, perseverance, and economy." This theme sat uncomfortably with the desperate struggles of most black Americans in the late 1800s. *Life and Times* sold only 463 copies in the first seven years after publication. In 1889, Douglass' publisher regretfully informed him that, although the firm had "pushed and repushed the book . . . interest in the days of slavery was not as great as we expected."

The same year, President Benjamin Harrison appointed Douglass as minister to Haiti. Haiti is a nation in the Caribbean that was an almost entirely dark-skinned one. In 1793, Toussaint L'Ouverture had begun the world's only successful slave revolt to liberate Haiti's people from their French slave owners. The United States wanted a naval base in the Caribbean. Douglass was supposed to help negotiate a lease for the magnificent harbor at Môle St. Nicholas, on the northwestern tip of Haiti. The negotiations failed, and Douglass resigned under pressure in 1891. American imperialists complained that he was too friendly with the Haitians and not forceful enough in negotiations.

Douglass' pride was hurt. In 1892, he found a Boston publisher to print a revised edition of *The Life and Times of Frederick Douglass*. Douglass hoped that his position as minister to Haiti might make people want to take another look at his career. He added more than 100 pages to the 1881 autobiography. The added pages included an eloquent call for civil rights and a long defense of his actions in Haiti. This edition sold only 399 copies in two years.

THE LAST CRUSADE

By the 1890s, the situation was desperate for black people in the South. African Americans were being lynched in growing numbers. White Southerners were burning the homes of African Americans and terrorizing their families just because they were demanding equal rights. Southern state legislatures passed so-called Jim Crow laws that segregated people by skin color. These laws were used to prevent African Americans from achieving economic and political equality with whites. The U.S. Supreme Court weakened the Fourteenth Amendment until it was almost useless. Whites in the South used literacy tests and poll taxes (per-person fees charged to voters) to keep blacks from voting. As black voters disappeared, so did black legislators, black sheriffs, and black jurors. The South became a white-run terror state.

The aging Douglass grew discouraged. "These ten or twelve years have not been cheerful," he wrote to an old abolitionist friend. "They have been years of reaction and darkness. . . . We have been . . . morally obscuring the difference between right and wrong."

In 1892, Douglass accepted an appointment as commissioner of the Republic of Haiti Pavilion at the 1893 World's Columbian Exposition, a world's fair in Chicago. In this position, he became friendly with Ida B. Wells. Wells was a black feminist who fearlessly exposed the horrors of lynching. From 1889 to 1892, more than 600 people were lynched without a trial in the United States. In 1892, Wells published her famous pamphlet entitled *Southern Horrors: Lynch Law in All Its Phases*. This pamphlet showed how Southern whites used lynching to terrorize and intimidate blacks. Many Southern whites believed that African Americans could only be controlled by fear. To them, lynching was the most effective means of control.

Douglass was energized once more. He joined Wells' campaign against lynching and torture in the South. He delivered his last great speech, "The Lesson of the Hour," in the fall of 1893, in Detroit. Douglass' speech, which detailed the horrors of lynching, aroused great sympathy. As always, he attacked the U.S. government for failing to protect black rights in the South. "The Lesson of the Hour" was a magnificent success as a speech. No federal anti-lynching law was ever passed, however.

Cedar Hill was Douglass' home from 1877 until his death in 1895. Perched high atop a hilltop in Washington, D.C., Cedar Hill provided its owner a sweeping view of the U.S. Capitol and the Washington D.C. skyline. Today, Cedar Hill, now known as the Frederick Douglass National Historic Site, is one of the District's most cherished landmarks.

Douglass retained some optimism despite the difficulties of his last years. "My day has been a pleasant one," he decided. "My joys have far exceeded my sorrows and my friends have brought me far more than my enemies have taken from me." On February 20, 1895, the 77-year old Douglass attended a women's rights meeting in Washington, D.C. That night, he suffered a massive heart attack and died. He was buried in Rochester with his first wife, Anna, and his daughter Annie. Five state legislatures adopted resolutions of regret when he died.

At the end of his life, Douglass befriended the great black poet Paul Laurence Dunbar. Douglass called Dunbar "the most promising young colored man" in America. After Douglass' death, Dunbar wrote a 10-stanza poem as a eulogy. The fourth stanza reads:

And he was no soft-tongued apologist;
He spoke straight-forward, fearlessly uncowed;
The sunlight of his truth dispelled the mist
And set in bold relief each dark-hued cloud;
To sin and crime he gave their proper hue,
And hurled at evil what was evil's due.

"The Beautiful, Needful Thing"

Paul Laurence Dunbar's poem after Douglass' death was not his last mention of the black leader. In 1903, he wrote the poem "Douglass." In this 14-line poem, the mood was not cheerful. The poem began:

> Ah, Douglass, we have fall'n on evil days,
> Such days as thou, not even thou didst know . . .

Dunbar did not have much to celebrate. The racist counter-revolution had succeeded in the South. White terrorists prevented blacks from voting or exercising other civil rights. Most Southern blacks still owned no land. They remained poor sharecroppers, oppressed by white businesspeople, shopkeepers, and landowners. Jim Crow laws ruled the South. In 1896, the U.S. Supreme Court ruled, in *Plessy v. Ferguson,* that the segregation of people by skin color did not contradict the U.S. Constitution. This allowed whites to force African Americans to use separate and unequal schools and hospitals. America's black citizens had to endure the shame of separate water fountains, racially divided waiting rooms in train stations, and seats at the back of the bus. Thousands of Southern blacks moved to the North, where they found poverty, race riots, and ghettos— segregated neighborhoods. It is no wonder that Dunbar ends his poem by yearning for Douglass' voice "to give us comfort through the lonely dark."

Douglass' voice always had been a voice of hope. He never lost the typical nineteenth-century faith in progress and in the ultimate triumph of civilization. When the U.S. Supreme Court began to support racism in the South, Douglass predicted that future generations would criticize the court's decisions and overturn them.

It took about half a century, but Douglass' hope was justified. In 1954, the Supreme Court overturned the *Plessy* ruling in *Brown v. Board of Education of Topeka.* Jim Crow segregation laws were no longer legal in the United States. After years of struggle by Americans—black and white, famous and unknown—the racist laws of the South were swept away. In 1964, the Civil Rights Act made it illegal to discriminate in public places or in employment based on race or gender. The next year, the Voting Rights Act restored the ability of blacks to vote in the South. Racism did not magically disappear in the United States. The trend was certainly in the right direction, however.

At the end of his final autobiography, Douglass summarized his life. He noted that he had "lived several lives in one: first, the life of slavery; secondly, the life of a fugitive from slavery; thirdly, the life of comparative freedom; fourthly, the life of conflict and battle; and fifthly, the life of victory, if not complete, at least assured." The events of the 1900s destroyed most people's belief in progress. With regard to race relations in the United States,

Frederick Douglass dedicated his entire life to ensuring voters' rights for blacks, and his dream was finally realized in 1965. A year after President Lyndon B. Johnson and Martin Luther King Jr. signed the historic Civil Rights Act, the Voting Rights Act of 1965 restored the right for blacks to vote in the South.

however, Douglass came closer to predicting the future than did most others: "Victory, if not complete, at least assured."

"A USEFUL RELATION TO HIS DAY AND GENERATION"

Frederick Douglass stands as a towering figure in the history of the United States. He was one of the greatest personalities of the nineteenth century. His contributions to human freedom, dignity, and justice were immense. He stood for the best of American ideals. His favorite document was always the Declaration of Independence.

Douglass survived and escaped from slavery by using his own talent, courage, and strength of character. Through a sheer act of will, and against all odds, he educated himself. He then spent his life attacking racist notions about black people.

Douglass was not perfect. He could be arrogant and vain. Many people thought that he was too quick to take offense. "In all my experience of men," one longtime abolitionist observed, "I have never known one not insane so able and willing as he is, to magnify the smallest cause of discomfort or wounded self esteem into unsupportable talk of offense and dissatisfaction."

Douglass was impulsive and passionate. He often changed his positions. He was a dedicated Garrisonian who then rejected the Boston abolitionists. He was a pacifist, then a convert to the use of violence in self-defense, and finally a supporter of John Brown. He hated the Constitution and then worshipped it. He respected the Republican Party and then held it in contempt. He admired Abraham Lincoln, criticized him as a secret racist, and then contributed to the myth of the martyred president.

Through a lifetime of twists and turns, however, Douglass never backed away from a fight against racial injustice. He supported the liberal belief in the worth of each individual person, whether black or white, rich or poor, woman or man, Northerner or Southerner. He wanted only to make "the nation's life consistent with the nation's creed." Black people "ask no favors of their fellow-citizens," Douglass thundered. "They ask only what is due them under the Declaration of Independence and the Constitution of the United States."

At the end of his final autobiography, Douglass tried to draw some lessons from his life to pass on to other people. He assured his readers:

> that knowledge can be obtained under difficulties—that poverty may give place to competency . . . and that a way is open to welfare and happiness to all who will resolutely and

One of the first U.S. monuments to honor a person of color, the Frederick Douglass statue memorialized a man who was dedicated to securing equality for all people. Douglass' work and efforts have made him one of the most prominent figures in U.S. history, helping to extend his influence to future activists who fight against injustice.

wisely pursue that way—that neither slavery, stripes, imprisonment, nor proscription need extinguish self-respect, crush manly ambition, or paralyze effort—that no power outside of himself can prevent a man from sustaining an honorable character and a useful relation to his day and generation.

TIME MAKES ALL THINGS EVEN

Robert Hayden (1913–1980) was the first African-American to serve as poet laureate of the United States. Hayden often wrote poems about the world as an imperfect and oppressive place that still was moving toward the possibility of a glorious future of justice and freedom. It is no surprise that one of Hayden's most famous poems is entitled "Frederick Douglass."

When it is finally Ours, this freedom, this liberty, this beautiful
and terrible thing, needful to man as air,
usable as earth; when it belongs at last to all,
when it is truly instinct, brain matter, diastole, systole,
reflex action; when it is finally won; when it is more
than the gaudy mumbo jumbo of politicians;
this man this Douglass, this former slave, this Negro
beaten to his knees, exiled, visioning a world
where none is lonely, none hunted, alien,
this man, superb in love and logic, this man
shall be remembered. Oh, not with statues' rhetoric,
not with legends and poems and wreaths of bronze alone,
but with the lives grown out of his life, the lives
fleshing his dream of the beautiful, needful thing.

⚔ CHRONOLOGY ⚔

1818   Frederick Augustus Washington Bailey is born in Tuckahoe County, Maryland.

1824   Relocated to Lloyd Plantation at Wye River.

1825   Frederick's mother dies.

1826   Sent to Hugh Auld's family in Baltimore; begins to learn to read; Aaron Anthony dies.

1827   Valuation of Anthony estate; Frederick inherited by Thomas Auld and sent to Baltimore.

1831   Obtains copy of *The Columbian Orator.*

1833   Moved back to St. Michaels to live with Thomas Auld.

1834   Spends year with "slave-breaker" Edward Covey.

1835   Spends year with William Freeland.

1836   Attempted escape foiled; returned to Hugh Auld in Baltimore.

1836-1838   Works in Baltimore shipyards as caulker; meets Anna Murray.

1838   Escapes north by train and boat; marries Anna Murray in New York City; settles in New Bedford, Massachusetts; takes name Frederick Douglass.

1839   Daughter Rosetta born (first child); subscribes to *The Liberator;* hears William Lloyd Garrison speak.

1840   Son Lewis Henry born (second child).

1841   Makes antislavery speeches in Nantucket, Massachusetts; meets William Lloyd Garrison; hired as lecturer for Massachusetts Anti-Slavery Society; moves family to Lynn, Massachusetts.

1842   Son Frederick Jr. born (third child).

1843 Attacked by proslavery mob in Pendleton, Indiana; argues with Henry Highland Garnet over usefulness of slave violence.

1844 Son Charles Remond born (fourth child).

1845 Publishes *Narrative of the Life of Frederick Douglass.*

1845-1847 Speaking tour of England, Scotland, and Ireland; British supporters raise money to purchase Douglass' freedom.

1847 Returns to the United States; moves to Rochester, New York; begins publication of the *North Star*; meets John Brown for the first time.

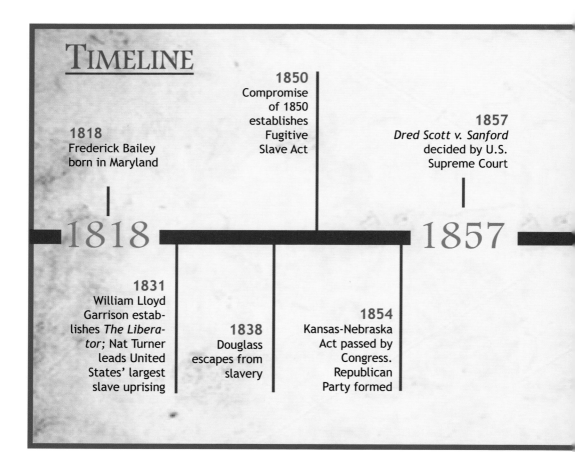

TIMELINE

1850
Compromise of 1850 establishes Fugitive Slave Act

1818
Frederick Bailey born in Maryland

1857
Dred Scott v. Sanford decided by U.S. Supreme Court

1818   **1857**

1831
William Lloyd Garrison establishes *The Liberator*; Nat Turner leads United States' largest slave uprising

1838
Douglass escapes from slavery

1854
Kansas-Nebraska Act passed by Congress. Republican Party formed

1848 Attends Women's Rights Convention at Seneca Falls, New York; Julia Griffiths moves from England to help with the *North Star*.

1849 Daughter Annie born (fifth and last child).

1851 Agrees with Gerrit Smith that U.S. Constitution is antislavery document; breaks openly with Garrison; the *North Star* renamed *Frederick Douglass' Paper*; supports Liberty Party.

1855 *My Bondage and My Freedom* published.

1856 Befriends Ottilie Assing, a German journalist.

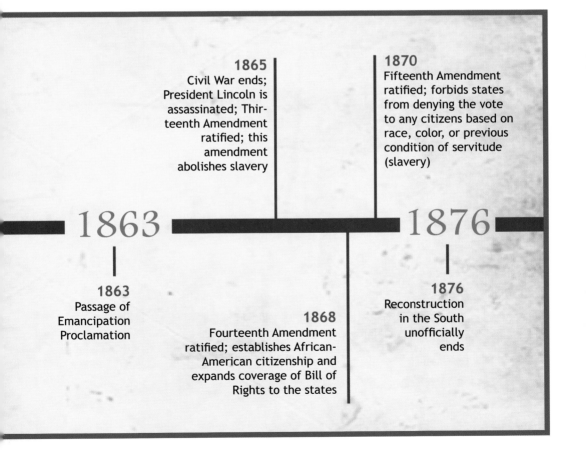

1865
Civil War ends; President Lincoln is assassinated; Thirteenth Amendment ratified; this amendment abolishes slavery

1870
Fifteenth Amendment ratified; forbids states from denying the vote to any citizens based on race, color, or previous condition of servitude (slavery)

1863

1876

1863
Passage of Emancipation Proclamation

1868
Fourteenth Amendment ratified; establishes African-American citizenship and expands coverage of Bill of Rights to the states

1876
Reconstruction in the South unofficially ends

1859   Declines to join John Brown's raid on Harpers Ferry, Virginia; flees to England to avoid possible arrest; begins publishing *Douglass' Monthly.*

1860   Daughter Annie dies; returns to United States; Abraham Lincoln elected president; South Carolina secedes from United States.

1861   Confederates open fire on Fort Sumter; Civil War begins.

1863   Emancipation Proclamation takes effect; recruits members for 54th Massachusetts, a black regiment in Union Army; first meeting with President Lincoln.

1864   Second meeting with President Lincoln.

1865   Criticizes President Andrew Johnson's soft Reconstruction plans; demands voting rights for freed people; Thirteenth Amendment to U.S. Constitution abolishes slavery.

1869   Breaks with feminist leaders over Fifteenth Amendment.

1870-1874   Publishes and edits Washington, D.C.–based *New National Era.*

1871   Appointed to Santo Domingo commission.

1872   Arson fire destroys Douglass' Rochester, New York, home; moves to Washington, D.C.

1874   Named president of Freedmen's Bank; bank fails.

1877   Appointed marshal for Washington, D.C., by President Rutherford B. Hayes; purchases Cedar Hill in Anacostia, D.C.

1881   Appointed recorder of deeds for Washington, D.C., by President James Garfield.

1882   Anna Douglass dies.

1884	Marries Helen Pitts.
1885—1887	Visits Europe and North Africa with wife.
1889	Appointed minister to Haiti by President Benjamin Harrison.
1891	Resigns as minister to Haiti.
1893-1894	Attacks white lynchings of blacks in the South.
1895	Dies at Cedar Hill.
1962	Cedar Hill added to U.S. National Park system.
1988	Cedar Hill declared a National Historic Site.

GLOSSARY

abolitionism   Before the Civil War (1861–1865), a movement to end slavery in the United States.

Burned-over district   An area in central and western New York, including Frederick Douglass' home city of Rochester, that was famous from 1820 to 1860 for its reform and radical politics.

colonization   A movement backed by some whites in the nineteenth century that supported emancipation as long as the freed slaves left the United States and went to Africa or the Caribbean.

Columbian Orator, The   A collection of political essays, poems, and dialogues, first published in 1797. It was widely used in American schoolrooms in the early 1800s. The book gave examples of speeches for students to copy and imitate. Douglass used this book to learn to read and speak.

Eastern Shore   An area of Maryland; a long peninsula between the Atlantic Ocean and Chesapeake Bay.

emigrationism   A movement backed by some blacks in the nineteenth and twentieth centuries; emigrationists concluded that white racism would never end in the United States, and blacks would be better off moving to some other country.

Free-Soil Party   Minor political party in the United States, active between 1848 and 1854; the party opposed the expansion of slavery into the western territories acquired in the Mexican American War.

Fugitive Slave Act   Law passed by the U.S. Congress as part of the Compromise of 1850. The law provided southern slaveholders with unfair legal weapons to use to capture slaves who had escaped to free states. The law threatened the rights of free African Americans and was extremely unpopular in the North.

lynching   A hanging or other form of execution carried out by a mob without a trial. In the United States, lynching usually refers to the murder of blacks by whites.

miscegenation   The "mixing" of different "races"; that is, marrying, having sexual relations, or having children with a partner from outside one's racially or ethnically defined group. In the United States, the term usually refers to African Americans ("blacks") and European Americans ("whites").

narrative   A type of writing that tells a story. It has a narrator who addresses someone, usually the reader. Douglass' autobiographies were examples of narratives.

Reconstruction   A period in U.S. history from approximately 1863 to 1876, when the U.S. government tried to solve the problems brought about by the end of the Civil War, especially the role and rights of freed African Americans in the South.

Stalwarts   A faction of the Republican Party in the 1870s and 1880s. The Stalwarts typically supported African-American rights in the South and opposed civil service reform. Frederick Douglass was a Stalwart Republican.

Underground Railroad   The system of secret routes used by people escaping from slavery in the South and traveling to the Northern states or to Canada.

BIBLIOGRAPHY

Andrews, William L., ed. *Critical Essays on Frederick Douglass.* Boston: G.K. Hall, 1991.

Andrews, William L. *To Tell a Free Story: The First Century of Afro American Autobiography, 1760–1865.* Urbana: University of Illinois Press, 1986.

Appiah, Kwame Anthony, and Martin Bunzl, eds. *Buying Freedom: The Ethics and Economics of Slave Redemption.* Princeton, NJ: Princeton University Press, 2007.

Bennett, Michael. *Democratic Discourses: The Radical Abolition Movement and Antebellum American Literature.* New Brunswick, NJ: Rutgers University Press, 2005.

Bloom, Harold, ed. *Frederick Douglass' Narrative of the Life of Frederick Douglass.* New York: Chelsea House, 1988.

Blue, Frederick J. *The Free Soilers: Third Party Politics, 1848–1854.* Urbana: University of Illinois Press, 1973.

———. *No Taint of Compromise: Crusaders in Antislavery Politics.* Baton Rouge: Louisiana State University Press, 2005.

Booraem, Hendrik. *The Formation of the Republican Party in New York: Politics and Conscience in the Antebellum North.* New York: New York University Press, 1983.

Bush, Harold K. Jr. *American Declarations: Rebellion and Repentance in American Cultural History.* Urbana: University of Illinois Press, 1999.

Carton, Evan. *Patriotic Treason: John Brown and the Soul of America.* New York: Free Press, 2006.

Davis, Charles T., and Henry Louis Gates Jr., eds. *The Slave's Narrative.* New York: Oxford University Press, 1985.

Davis, Reginald F. *Frederick Douglass: A Precursor of Liberation Theology*. Macon, GA: Mercer University Press, 2005.

D'Entremont, John. *Southern Emancipator: Moncure Conway, The American Years, 1832–1865*. New York: Oxford University Press, 1987.

Diedrich, Maria. *Love Across Color Lines: Ottilie Assing & Frederick Douglass*. New York: Hill and Wang, 1999.

Douglass, Frederick. *The Frederick Douglass Papers. Series One: Speeches, Debates, and Interviews*. John W. Blassingame, ed. 5 volumes. New Haven, Conn.: Yale University Press, 1979–1992.

———. *The Frederick Douglass Papers. Series Two: Autobiographical Writings*. John W. Blassingame, ed. 2 volumes. New Haven, Conn.: Yale University Press, 1999– .

———. *Life and Times of Frederick Douglass* (rev. ed., 1892). New York: Collier, 1962.

Douglass, Frederick. *The Life and Writings of Frederick Douglass*. Philip S. Foner, ed. New York, International Publishers, 1950.

Fields, Barbara Jeanne. *Slavery and Freedom on the Middle Ground: Maryland during the Nineteenth Century*. New Haven, Conn.: Yale University Press, 1985.

Finkelman, Paul. *Dred Scott v. Sandford: A Brief History with Documents*. Boston: Bedford Books, 1997.

Foner, Philip S., and George E. Walker, eds. *Proceedings of the Black State Conventions, 1840–1865*. 2 vols. Philadelphia: Temple University Press, 1979–1980.

Foster, Frances Smith. *Witnessing Slavery: The Development of Ante-Bellum Slave Narratives*. Madison: University of Wisconsin Press, 1994.

Friedman, Lawrence J. *Gregarious Saints: Self and Community in Antebellum American Abolitionism, 1830–1870*. New York: Cambridge University Press, 1982.

Garrison, William Lloyd. *The Letters of William Lloyd Garrison: From Disunionism to the Brink of War, 1850–1860*. 6 vols. Walter Merrill and Louis Ruchames, eds. Cambridge, Mass.: Harvard University Press, 1971–1981.

Harrold, Stanley. *American Abolitionists*. Harlow, UK: Pearson Education Limited, 2001.

Jeffrey, Julie Roy. *The Great Silent Army of Abolitionism: Ordinary Women in the Antislavery Movement*. Chapel Hill: University of North Carolina Press, 1998.

Laurie, Bruce. *Beyond Garrison: Antislavery and Social Reform*. New York: Cambridge University Press, 2005.

Lawson, Bill E., and Frank M. Kirkland. *Frederick Douglass: A Critical Reader*. Malden, Mass.: Blackwell, 1999.

Lee, Maurice S. *Slavery, Philosophy, & American Literature, 1830–1860*. New York: Cambridge University Press, 2005.

Levine, Robert S. *Martin Delany, Frederick Douglass, and the Politics of Representative Identity*. Chapel Hill, NC: University of North Carolina Press, 1997.

Martin, Waldo E. Jr. *The Mind of Frederick Douglass*. Chapel Hill, NC: University of North Carolina Press, 1984.

Mayfield, John. *Rehearsal for Republicanism: Free Soil and the Politics of Antislavery*. Port Washington, NY: Kennikat Press, 1980.

McDowell, Deborah E., and Arnold Rampersad, eds. *Slavery and the Literary Imagination*. Baltimore, MD: Johns Hopkins University Press, 1989.

McFeely, William S. *Frederick Douglass*. New York: W.W. Norton, 1991.

Newman, Richard, Patrick Rael, and Phillip Lapsansky, eds. *Pamphlets of Protest: An Anthology of Early African American Protest Literature, 1790–1860*. New York: Routledge, 2001.

Oakes, James. *The Radical and the Republican: Frederick Douglass, Abraham Lincoln, and the Triumph of Antislavery*. New

York: W.W. Norton, 2007.

Oates, Stephen B. *To Purge This Land with Blood: A Biography of John Brown*. Amherst: University of Massachusetts Press, 1984.

Phillips, Wendell. *Speeches, Lectures, and Letters by Wendell Phillips*. Boston: James Redpath, 1863.

Preston, Dickson J. *Young Frederick Douglass: The Maryland Years*. Baltimore, MD: Johns Hopkins University Press, 1980.

Quarles, Benjamin. *Allies for Freedom* (1974) and *Blacks on John Brown* (1972). Cambridge, Mass.: Da Capo Press. Reissued together in 2001.

——. *Black Abolitionists*. New York: Oxford University Press, 1969.

——. "Introduction," in Frederick Douglass, *Narrative of the Life of Frederick Douglass* . . . Cambridge, Mass.: Harvard University Press, 1960.

Renehan, Edward J. Jr. *The Secret Six: The True Tale of the Men Who Conspired with John Brown*. Columbia: University of South Carolina Press, 1997.

Reynolds, David S. *John Brown, Abolitionist: The Man Who Killed Slavery, Sparked the Civil War, and Seeded Civil Rights*. New York: Alfred A. Knopf, 2005.

Riss, Arthur. *Race, Slavery, and Liberalism in Nineteenth-century American Literature*. New York: Cambridge University Press, 2006.

Robertson, Stacey M. *Parker Pillsbury: Radical Abolitionist, Male Feminist*. Ithaca, NY: Cornell University Press, 2000.

"Rochester Ladies' Anti-Slavery Society: Records, 1851–1868." University of Michigan. Available online at http://www.clements.umich.edu/Webguides/QR/Rochester.html.

Rossbach, Jeffrey S. *Ambivalent Conspirators: John Brown, the Secret Six, and a Theory of Slave Violence*. Philadelphia: University of Pennsylvania Press, 1982.

Sernett, Milton C. *Abolition's Axe: Beriah Green, Oneida Institute, and the Black Freedom Struggle*. Syracuse, NY: Syracuse University Press, 1986.

———. *North Star Country: Upstate New York and the Crusade for African American Freedom*. Syracuse, NY: Syracuse University Press, 2002.

Stauffer, John. *The Black Hearts of Men: Radical Abolitionists and the Transformation of Race*. Cambridge, Mass.: Harvard University Press, 2001.

Stewart, James Brewer. *Holy Warriors: The Abolitionists and American Slavery*. New York: Hill and Wang, 1976.

Strong, Douglas M. *Perfectionist Politics: Abolitionism and the Religious Tensions of American Democracy*. Syracuse, NY: Syracuse University Press, 1999.

Walters, Ronald G. *The Antislavery Appeal: American Abolitionism after 1830*. Baltimore, MD: Johns Hopkins University Press, 1976.

Wade, Richard C. *Slavery in the Cities: The South, 1820–1860* London: Oxford University Press, 1964.

Warren, James Perrin. *Culture of Eloquence: Oratory and Reform in Antebellum America*. University Park: Pennsylvania State University Press, 1999.

Waters, Carver Wendell. *Voice in the Slave Narratives of Olaudah Equiano, Frederick Douglass, and Solomon Northup*. Lewiston, NY: Edwin Mellen Press, 2002.

Wyatt-Brown, Bertram. *Lewis Tappan and the Evangelical War against Slavery*. Cleveland, OH: The Press of Case Western Reserve University, 1969.

Yacovone, Donald. *Samuel Joseph May and the Dilemmas of the Liberal Persuasion, 1797–1871*. Philadelphia: Temple University Press, 1991.

FURTHER RESOURCES

Altman, Linda Jacobs. *Slavery and Abolition in American History*. Berkeley Heights, NJ: Enslow Publishers, 1999.

Douglass, Frederick. *Narrative of the Life of Frederick Douglass, An American Slave, Written by Himself*. Boston, 1845.

Greenidge, Kerri. *Boston's Abolitionists*. Beverly, Mass.: Commonwealth Editions, 2006.

McArthur, Debra. *The Kansas-Nebraska Act and "Bleeding Kansas" in American History*. Berkeley Heights, NJ: Enslow Publishers, 2003.

McFeely, William S. *Frederick Douglass*. New York: W.W. Norton, 1991.

McNeese, Tim. *Dred Scott v. Sandford: The Pursuit of Freedom*. New York: Chelsea House, 1997.

McPherson, James. *Battle Cry of Freedom: The Civil War Era*. New York: Oxford University Press, 1988.

Sterngass, Jon. *John Brown*. New York: Chelsea House, 2008.

WEB SITES

American Visionaries: Frederick Douglass
http://www.nps.gov/history/museum/exhibits/douglass/
An image gallery with information about Frederick Douglass with photographs of items that he owned.

Douglass, Frederick. *Narrative of the Life of Frederick Douglass, An American Slave, Written by Himself*
http://sunsite.berkeley.edu/Literature/Douglass/Autobiography/
Frederick Douglass' first autobiography.

Frederick Douglass National Historic Site
  http://www.nps.gov/frdo

  This site is sponsored by the National Park Service and features a virtual tour of Frederick Douglass' home.

The Frederick Douglass Papers at the Library of Congress
  http://memory.loc.gov/ammem/doughtml/doughome.html

  The Library of Congress Manuscript Division contains approximately 7,400 items (38,000 images) relating to Frederick Douglass' life.

The Gerrit Smith Virtual Museum
  http://www.nyhistory.com/gerritsmith/index.htm

  A site about the life of Gerrit Smith.

Harpers Ferry National Historical Park
  http://www.nps.gov/archive/hafe/home.htm

  The history of Harpers Ferry and the people who left their mark.

To Be More Than Equal: The Many Lives of Martin R. Delany, 1812–1885
  http://www.libraries.wvu.edu/delany/home.htm

  A site about the life of Martin R. Delany.

WWW-VL: Coming of the Civil War, 1850–1860: The Pre-Civil War Years in United States History
  http://www.vlib.us/eras/war.htm

  The history of the United States before the American Civil War.

PICTURE CREDITS

INDEX

slaves/slavery
  abolished, 104–105, 110
  attempts to overthrow, 96, 99
  in cities, 36
  cotton and, 10–12
  in Deep South, 21, 25, 33
  disbelief in Douglass as for-
    mer, 55, 56, 60
  Dred Scott decision and, 94
  education of, 24–26
  Fourth of July and, 90–91
  fugitive, 41–43, 85–86, 93
  hired out, 28, 29, 33, 36–37
  Lincoln and, 102, 104–105,
    108, 109
  in Maryland, 24–25, 37–38
  in North, 12
  population of, 13, 24, 25, 37,
    45
  Republican Party and, 101
  in territories from Mexico,
    84–85
  treatment of, 12–13, 20–21,
    29
  treatment of Douglass as, 20,
    22–23, 65–68
  See also abolitionist(s)
Smith, Gerrit
  American Abolition Society
    and, 90
  background of, 86–87
  Douglass and, 87, 89
  home of, 74
  as presidential candidate, 100
South
  after Civil War, 110, 113–114,
    127–128, 131–132
  cotton and, 10–12
  free blacks in, 13
  See also slaves/slavery
Southern Horrors: Lynch Law in

All Its Phases (Wells), 128
Stanton, Elizabeth Cady, 54, 81,
  83, 114
Stowe, Harriet Beecher, 86, 90
suffrage
  for African Americans after
    Civil War, 111, 112–113,
    127, 132
  for free blacks, 76
  for women, 80, 81, 83, 114–
    115

T
Tappan, Arthur and Lewis, 47
tobacco, 24
Turner, Nat, 96

U
Uncle Tom's Cabin (Stowe), 86
Underground Railroad, 41–43,
  71, 93
U.S. Constitution, 50, 79, 87,
  110, 112–113, 128
U.S. Supreme Court, 94–95,
  112, 127, 132

V
Van Buren, Martin, 80
Voting Rights Act (1965), 132

W
Walker, David, 96
Washington, D.C., 115, 122
Wells, Ida B., 128
women
  in abolition movement, 48
  Douglass and strong, 126
  rights of, 80, 81, 83, 114–115
Women's Rights Convention
  (1848), 81, 83
Wye House, 17–20, 67, 68

⚔ ABOUT THE AUTHOR ⚔

JON STERNGASS is the author of *First Resorts: Pursuing Pleasure at Saratoga Springs, Newport, and Coney Island*. He is a freelance writer who specializes in children's nonfiction books. He has written more than 30 books; his most recent works are a biography of John Brown and a history of Filipino-Americans. Born and raised in Brooklyn, New York, Sterngass has a B.A. in history from Franklin and Marshall College, an M.A. in medieval history from the University of Wisconsin–Milwaukee, and a Ph.D. in nineteenth-century American history from The City University of New York. He has lived in Saratoga Springs, New York, for 16 years with his wife, Karen Weltman, and sons Eli (15) and Aaron (12). Frederick Douglass was one of Sterngass's childhood heroes, and he enjoyed the opportunity to revisit Cedar Hill with his family.